アメリカのホテル
＆そのレストラン
AMERICAN HOTELS & THEIR RESTAURANTS

斎 藤 武

アメリカのホテル ＆そのレストラン
AMERICAN HOTELS & THEIR RESTAURANTS

目次
CONTENTS

●目次／Contents

☆ **CALIFORNIA**

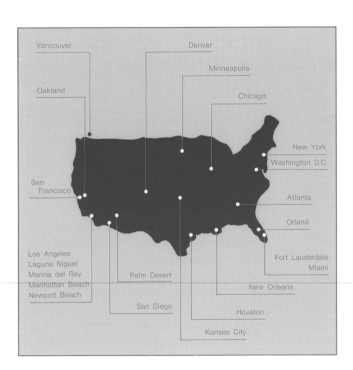

はじめに

ホテルがチェーン展開する場合デザイン的に統一されたものが主であり、それは1970年前半まで続いた。しかし、1966年ジョン・ポートマンが「ハイアット」にアトリウムを取り入れてからは全く新しい傾向が現れはじめ、ホテルデザインの個性化と多様性が考えられるようになった。

80年代になり、立地やライフスタイルの変化、利用客のニーズに応じているいろな要素や形が、ホテルに反映されるようになってきた。

たとえば、エグゼクティブ・ビジネスマンを対象としたホテルでは、上得意のメンバーを中心に宿泊させ、あらゆるサービスに対応できるクラブフロアと専用ラウンジを設けている。また、ビジネスセンターや、ヘルシー志向によるアスレチックセンター、ディスコ・パブの設置などが、最近のホテル施設の流行でもある。

一方、低料金のホテルとしてこれらの設備を省き宿泊のみを目的とした"バジェット・ホテル""エコノミーホテル"。長期滞在型のホテルとしてキッチンが各部屋にそなえつけられた"スイート・ホテル"。チェーンではなくアメニティを含むサービスでより個性を強調する客にターゲットをしぼった"ブティック・ホテル"。大規模なコンベンションやリゾート施設を備えよりライフスタイルをエンジョイさせるためのホテルなど新しい傾向のホテルが出現している。

レストラン施設においては、メインダイニングがフランス料理中心からその重厚な雰囲気を保ちながらも、イタリアや新しいアメリカ料理の導入など、カジュアル化が進んでいる。

本書では、1980年代にオープンしたアメリカとカナダのホテルから、バラエティに富み話題の30軒をセレクト。そのロビー・フロントレセプション・バー&ラウンジ・会議室・宴会場・客室・レストランやヘルスクラブ・フィットネスクラブ・スポーツ施設など併せて収録した。本書から最新の"アメリカのホテル&そのレストラン"の動きを読み取っていただければ幸いである。

最後に、本書をまとめるにあたり、週刊「ホテル&レストラン」月刊「ザ・ホテル」月刊「飲食店経営」アメリカの業界誌「Hotels & Restaurants International」の各編集部、マデリン M.シュナイター及び関係各位の協力に感謝します。

1988年5月　　　　　　　　　　　斎藤　武

FOREWORD

As the development of hotels occurs within a chain, many of them feature traditionally a common design, and this tendency had continued by the first half of the 70's. However, since John Portman introduced an atrium in "Hyatt" in 1966, a quite new tendency took place, giving a new value to individualization and diversification in hotel design.

In the 80's, along with changes in location, life-style and guest needs, various elements and forms have been proposed for hotel design.

For example, hotels catering mainly for executives and businessmen accept also other customers, and they are provided with club floor and special lounges to satisfy any service requirements, a business center, an athletic center for health-conscious customers, a disco, pub, etc. Installing these facilities is a recent trend in the hotel world.

"Budget hotels" and "economy hotels" that are not equipped with those facilities are cheap, and they cater for only those who stay. Intended for customers with longer period of stay are "suite hotels" where each guest room is equipped with a kitchen. "Boutique hotels" are not developed as a chain, but they are intended for guests who are oriented toward individuality, by offering hospitable services, including amenities. There are also hotels with large convention halls, resrot facilities, etc. to allow guests to enjoy a multifarious life-style. Thus, new-type hotels are appearing.

As for restaurant facilities, the so-called main dining is shifting from the one centering around French dishes to casual ones in which Italian and new American dishes are introduced while maintaining the dignified French atmosphere.

This book covers 30 hotels with a variety of topics selected from those that have opened in the U.S. and Canada in the 80's, with illustrations of their lobbies, front receptions, bars & lounges, boardrooms, banquet halls, and guest rooms, as well as health and fitness clubs, and sports facilities. The author will be more than pleased if readers can grasp through this work the latest trends of the "American hotels and their restaurants."

In closing, we would like to thank the editorial staffs of weekly "Hotel & Restaurant," monthly "The Hotel," monthly "Inshokuten Keiei," and American trade journal "Hotels & Restaurants International," Madelin M. Schneider, and others who have extended their precious cooperation.

May 1988

Gen Takeshi Saito

Published by **Shotenkenchiku-sha Co., Ltd.**
7-22-36-2, Nishi-shinjuku, Shinjuku-ku, Tokyo 160 Japan

別冊商店建築37 **アメリカのホテル&そのレストラン** 1988年6月20日発行

著者●斎藤　武　　　編集●辻田　博　　協力スタッフ
編集発行人●村上末吉　　制作●菅谷良夫　　表紙デザイン●ウィークエンド
　　　　　　　　　　　　　　　　　　　　本文レイアウト●ぱとおく社　　印刷●小堀製版印刷
　　　　　　　　　　　　　　　　　　　　英文●海広社　　写植●福島写植
　　　　　　　　　　　　　　　　　　　　　　　　　　　製本●坂田製本／山田製本

発行所　株式会社商店建築社 ©
本社　東京都新宿区西新宿7-22-36-2 〒160　TEL(03)363-5770代
支社　大阪市南区大宝寺西之町21 第3大京ビル 〒542　TEL(06)251-6523代
ISBN 4-7858-0098-4

世界的に有名な建築家John C.Portmanの設計による広大なアトリウムの中央部にグラス エレベーターが上下する

The 50-storied hotel designed by John C. Portman.

NEW YORK **Marriott**
MARQUIS

1535 Broadway New York, N.Y. 10019
Phone / 212-398-1900

50階建のホテルの正面は"妊娠した女性"というニックネームで親しまれている

The front design is affectionately called a "pregnant woman."

5

近代的なアトリウムを樹木の緑で自然を強調する

1階のエレベーターホール

"The Clook Lounge"（8階）樹木の下でカクテルが楽しめる　下のフロアは会議室と宴会場

8階のレセプション廻り

部屋のチェック インはこの長いレセプションでする

ストリート レベルにある大理石のエレベーターホール

6

"Atrium Café" の Built-in deli   Built-in deli at Atrium cafe.

"Atrium café"（84席）グリーンのカーペットとメロンカラーの調度類で構成されている

ゆったりとした椅子の "The Broadway Lounge"
The Broadway lounge with comfortable seats.

"The Broadway Lounge"（8階）　回転式のバーラウンジ　ブロードウエイ通りが見える

(Photo captions – page 6)
From left above:
● Nature is emphasized by fringing the modern atrium with trees.
● The elevator hall at the 1st floor.
● The reception area at the 8th floor.
● The room checkin is made at this long reception.
Right, top / The cook lounge (8th floor) – you can enjoy a cocktail under the trees.
Right, bottom / The elevator hall at the street level.

(Photo captions – page 7)
Left, top / Atrium cafe (84 seats).
Left, bottom / The Broadway lounge (8th floor).

ニューヨーク マリオット マーキー

「マリオットホテルズ アンド リゾート」のチェーンの中で最も規模の大きいホテル（50階建1876室）である。設計は1967年に完成したアトランタの「ハイアット リージェンシーホテル（Hyatt Regency Hotel）」のデザインで話題をさらって以来　多くのホテル建築を手掛けているJhon C.Portman氏である。

オープン アトリウムやグラス エレベーター　樹木や泉を取り入れた広大なロビーなどの彼独特の演出が　このホテルにも活かされている。

1972年に当時のN.Y.市長 John Lindsay を中心に　コンベンション都市としてより活気を促すために　どうしてもこのようなホテル施設が必要であるとし　ブロードウエイ再開発計画の一環として企画された。その実現のため　Portman氏に協力を働きかけ　途中財政的　保護主義者たち　空中権（Air rights）といった様々な問題をかかえながら　過去20年間におけるニューヨークで最も新しいデラックス コンベンションホテルとして登場し　話題となっている。

経営管理/Marriott Corporation, Washington D.C.

設計/John C.Portman & Associates, Atlanta

オープン/1985年10月10日

規模・客室数/50階建　1876室（内スイート141室）

その他の施設/Grand ballroom（28,800sq.-ft.）Junior
　　　　ballroom（6,120sq.-ft.）5th FL Ballroom/exhibit
　　　　hall（22,500sq.-ft.）Meeting room（41room）

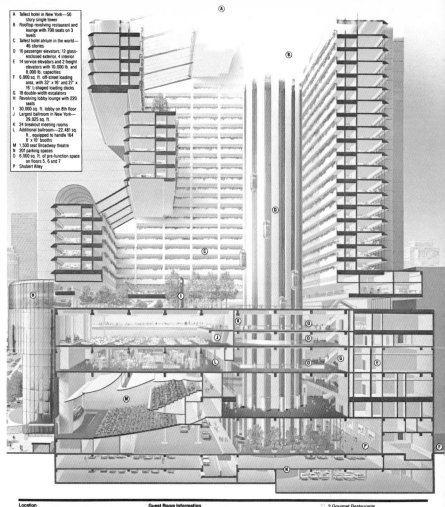

A Tallest hotel in New York—50 story single tower
B Rooftop revolving restaurant and lounge with 700 seats on 3 levels
C Tallest hotel atrium in the world—46 stories
D 16 passenger elevators; 12 glass-enclosed exterior, 4 interior
E 14 service elevators and 2 freight elevators with 10,000 lb. and 8,000 lb. capacities
F 6,000 sq. ft. off-street loading area, with 32' x 16' and 27' x 15' L-shaped loading docks
G 18 double-width escalators
H Revolving lobby lounge with 220 seats
I 30,000 sq. ft. lobby on 8th floor
J Largest ballroom in New York—29,025 sq. ft.
K 24 breakout meeting rooms
L Additional ballroom—22,481 sq. ft.; equipped to handle 164 8' x 10' booths
M 1,500 seat Broadway theatre
N 201 parking spaces
O 6,000 sq. ft. of pre-function space on floors 5, 6 and 7
P Shubert Alley

NEW YORK MARRIOTT MARQUIS

This is the largest hotel of the "Marriott Hotels & Resort" chain (50-storied, with 1,876 rooms). This building has been designed by Mr. John C. Portman who has designed also many other hotels, from the days he became well known for his design of "Hyatt Regency Hotel," Atlanta, whose construction had been completed in 1967.

For this hotel, too, his own unique presentation has been adopted, including an open atrium, glassed elevators and a spacious lobby arranged with trees, a fountain, etc.

In 1972, under the leadership of the former N.Y mayor John Lindsay who felt it absolutely necessary to provide this type of hotel facilities in order to promote New York as a convention city, the construction of this hotel has been planned as part of Broadway redevelopment program. Mr. Portman has been requested to cooperate in the realization of this hotel. While facing many problems, such as the financial protectionists' opposition and air rights, this hotel could be finally realized as the newest and most luxurious convention hotel in New York for the last 20 years.

1535 Broadway, New York, N.Y. 10019
Phone: 212-398-1900

Management & operation / Marriott Corporation, Washington D.C.
Design / John C. Portman & Associates, Inc., Atlanta
Opened / October 10, 1985
Scale, number of guest rooms / 50 stories, 1,876 rooms (incl. 141 suite rooms)
Other facilities / Grand ballroom (28,800 sq. ft.), Junior ballroom (6,120 sq. ft.) at 5th fl., Ballroom/exhibit hall (22,500 sq. ft.), Meeting rooms (41)

Two-floor lounges: The Broadway lounge at the 1st floor, and Promenade lounge at the 2nd floor.

Location
☐ On Broadway between 45th and 46th Streets, in the heart of the Theatre district.
☐ Nine blocks from the New York Convention Center

Meeting, Banquet and Exhibition Facilities
☐ 29,025 sq. ft. Grand Ballroom with 10 subdivisions
☐ 22,481 sq. ft. Ballroom Exhibition Hall with 11 subdivisions
☐ 6,055 sq. ft. Junior Ballroom with 2 subdivisions
☐ 24 additional meeting and conference rooms
☐ Over 18,000 sq. ft. of pre-function space
☐ 1,500 seat Broadway Theatre
☐ Separate banquet kitchen on Ballroom level

Guest Room Information
☐ 1,876 oversized guest rooms—13'7" x 21'
☐ 985 double doubles (floors 10-45)
☐ 648 kings (floors 10-45)
☐ 25 parlors (one per full floor)
☐ 101 concierge rooms with separate check-in and check-out (floors 30 and 31)
☐ 141 suites: 82 with wet bars (floors 16, 17, 23, 24, 37, 38, 43, 44 and 45)
☐ 2 Presidential and 2 Vice Presidential Suites (Floors 44 and 45)
☐ 40 handicapped accessible rooms

Dining and Entertainment
☐ Three-level rooftop revolving restaurant and lounge
☐ Lobby-level revolving lounge

☐ 2 Gourmet Restaurants
☐ 2 Lobby Lounges
☐ 2 Coffee Shops

Recreation/Guest Facilities
☐ Health Club with Jacuzzi, Saunas, Exercise Room and Juice Bar
☐ 15,000 sq. ft. of retail shops
☐ Airline, Car Rental and Tour Desks
☐ Giftshop/Newsstand
☐ Commercial airport transportation
☐ Taxi stand
☐ Every facility is handicapped accessible

2階構成のラウンジ　1階が"The Broadway Lounge"　2階が"Promenade Lounge"

4TH FLOOR

Meeting Room	Dimensions (W x L x H)	Square Footage	Theater	Schoolroom	Conference	U-Shape	Reception	Banquet
Boardroom 1	22'x21'x10'	462	60	25	20	20	75	40
Boardroom 2	28'x21'x10'	588	80	35	26	26	95	60
Boardroom 3	29'x21'x10'	609	80	35	28	28	100	60
Boardroom 4	27'x21'x10'	567	75	30	26	26	90	60
Boardrooms 3 + 4	56'x21'x10'	1176	155	95	52	52	190	100
Boardroom 5	28'x21'x10'	588	80	35	26	26	95	60
Boardroom 6	29'x21'x10'	609	80	35	28	28	100	60
Boardroom 7	28'x23'x10'	644	85	35	30	30	105	60
Boardroom 8	28'x23'x10'	644	85	35	30	30	105	60
Boardroom 9	29'x23'x10'	667	90	35	30	30	105	60
Boardrooms 8 + 9	57'x23'x10'	1311	175	105	58	58	210	120
Boardroom 10	28'x23'x10'	644	85	35	30	30	105	60
Boardroom 11	23'x23'x10'	529	70	30	24	24	85	40

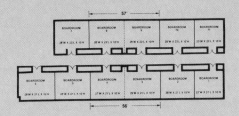

5TH FLOOR

Meeting Room	Dimensions (W x L x H)	Square Footage	Theater	Schoolroom	Conference	U-Shape	Reception	Banquet
Ballroom Exhibition Hall	182'x124'x12'2"	22,481	3050	1800	—	—	3500	2200
North	90'x124'x12'2"	10,872	1450	870	—	—	1725	1080
Center(plus corridor)	65'x124'x12'2"	8,060	1075	645	—	—	1275	720
Center	54'x124'x12'2"	6,696	900	535	—	—	1075	600
Meeting Rms 1-4	35'x116'x10'	4,176	550	335	—	—	650	330
Meeting Rm 1	26'x25'x10'	650	85	39	28	28	100	50
Meeting Rm 2	28'x25'x10'	700	95	42	30	30	110	60
Meeting Rm 3	28'x25'x10'	700	95	42	30	30	110	60
Meeting Rm 4	31'x25'x10'	775	105	45	34	34	125	60
South	90'x124'x12'2"	11,952	1600	955	—	—	1900	1080
Center(plus corridor)	65'x124'x12'2"	8,060	1075	645	—	—	1275	720
Center	54'x124'x12'2"	6,696	900	535	—	—	1075	600
Meeting Rms 5-9	35'x146'x10'	5,256	700	420	—	—	825	420
Meeting Rm 5	33'x25'x10'	825	110	48	36	36	130	60
Meeting Rm 6	28'x25'x10'	700	95	42	30	30	110	60
Meeting Rm 7	28'x25'x10'	700	95	42	30	30	110	60
Meeting Rm 8	28'x25'x10'	700	95	42	30	30	110	60
Meeting Rm 9	26'x25'x10'	650	85	39	28	28	100	50
Center(plus corridor)	130'x124'x12'2"	16,120	2175	1275	—	—	2575	1560
Center	108'x124'x12'2"	13,392	1800	1075	—	—	2125	1200

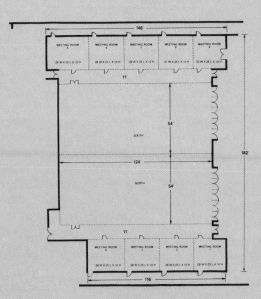

Ballroom Exhibition Hall

Size: 22,481 sq. ft.

Ceiling Height
Center: 12'2"
Side Sections: 10'

Sound
Microphone jack in each subdivision
Local and remote sound controls in each subdivision
Volume control in each subdivision

Electric
60 amp, 120V - 208V, three phase four wire outlets in each subdivision and on columns
200 amp, 120V - 208V, three phase four wire plug in bussduct in center ceiling

20 amp outlet in each subdivision and on columns
Incandescent lighting with full-range dimming capabilities
Fixed light level high intensity discharge lighting

Water and Drain
Six utility boxes located in floor of center section with hot and cold water and drain

Floor Load Capacity
163 lbs. per sq. ft.

Telephone
Jack in each subdivision

T.V.
Jack in each subdivision

Booth Capabilities
164 8' x 10'; 130 10' x 10'

6TH FLOOR

Meeting Room	Dimensions (W x L x H)	Square Footage	Theater	Schoolroom	Conference	U-Shape	Reception	Banquet
Grand Ballroom	Irregular	29,025	3500	2050	—	—	3500	2500
North	87'x118'x23'	10,266	1375	820	—	—	1625	960
Center(plus corridor)	67'x118'x23'	7,906	1075	625	—	—	1250	720
Center	52'x118'x23'	6,136	825	490	—	—	975	600
Salons A-D	35'x101'10	3,535	475	280	—	—	550	300
Salon A	20'x20'x10'	400	50	24	18	18	60	40
Salon B	27'x20'x10'	540	70	30	24	24	85	50
Salon C	26'x20'x10'	520	70	30	24	24	80	50
Salon D	29'x20'x10'	580	75	33	26	26	90	60
South	87'x118'x23'	10,266	1375	820	—	—	1625	960
Center(plus corridor)	67'x118'x23'	7,906	1075	625	—	—	1250	720
Center	52'x118'x23'	6,136	825	490	—	—	975	600
Salons E-H	35'x101'x10'	3,535	475	280	—	—	550	300
Salon E	29'x20'x10'	580	75	33	26	26	90	60
Salon F	26'x20'x10'	520	70	30	24	24	80	50
Salon G	27'x20'x10'	540	70	30	24	24	85	50
Salon H	20'x20'x10'	400	50	24	18	18	60	40
Center(plus corridor)	134'x118'x23'	15,812	2150	1250	—	—	2500	1560
Center	104'x118'x23'	12,272	1650	980	—	—	1950	1200

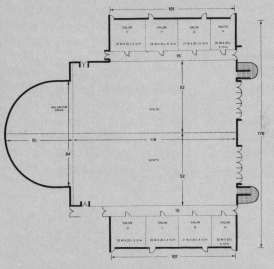

Grand Ballroom

Size: 29,025 sq. ft.

Ceiling Height
Center: 23'
Side Section: 10'

Sound
Control room above the 7th floor balcony
Control panels in front of stage and in each subdivision
Microphone jack in each subdivision
Local and remote sound controls in each subdivision
Volume control in each subdivision

Electric
60 amp, 120V - 208V, three phase four wire outlets in each subdivision and on columns

20 amp outlet in each subdivision and on columns
Incandescent lighting with full-range dimming capabilities
Lighting control room above 7th floor balcony
Lighting control panel in front of stage and in each subdivision

Floor Load Capacity
163 lbs. per sq. ft.

Telephone
Jack in each subdivision

T.V.
Jack in each subdivision

Booth Capabilities
164 8' x 10'; 130 10' x 10'

7TH FLOOR

Meeting Room	Dimensions (W x L x H)	Square Footage	Theater	Schoolroom	Conference	U-Shape	Reception	Banquet
7th Flr. Balcony	Irregular	5,596	550	325	—	—	—	500
Junior Ballroom	53'x134'x10'	6,055	800	475	—	—	950	500
Pre-function	29'x46'x10'	1,553	200	120	—	—	245	100
Ballroom	53'x86'x10'	4,437	600	355	—	—	700	400
Meeting RM 1	30'x25'x10'	750	100	45	33	33	120	60
Meeting RM 2	30'x17'x10'	510	70	30	22	22	80	40
Meeting RMS 1, 2	42'x30'x10'	1,260	170	100	56	56	200	120
Meeting RM 3	29'x22'x10'	638	85	35	27	27	100	60
Meeting RM 4	28'x22'x10'	616	85	35	28	28	95	60
Meeting RM 5	26'x22'x10'	572	75	30	25	25	90	50
Meeting RMS 3, 4, 5	83'x22'x10'	1,826	245	145	82	82	290	160
Meeting RM 6	26'x25'x10'	650	90	35	29	29	100	50
Meeting RM 7	27'x24'x10'	648	90	35	29	29	100	50
Meeting RM 8	27'x22'x10'	594	80	35	26	26	95	50
Meeting RM 9	24'x22'x10'	528	70	30	24	24	80	40
Meeting RM 10	28'x22'x10'	616	85	35	28	28	95	60
Meeting RMS 8, 9, 10	79'x22'x10'	1,738	235	135	78	78	275	160

"Encore" 24時間営業のカジュアル レストラン

"Encore"—a casual restaurant open for 24 hours.

朝 昼 夜と店内のセットが変わる

The inside set changes between morning, daytime and night.

店内中央部の円形ビュッフェ

A round buffet in the center.

サービスワゴンとテーブルセッティング

"JW's Restaurant"（84席）同ホテルのグルメ レストランは バーとダイニングエリアで構成
"JW's Restaurant" (84 seats) – this hotel's gourmet restaurant consists of bar and dining.

壁面デザインとしてのワインセラー

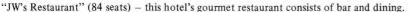

ロビーレベルのギフトショップ

バーエリアより店内をみる　　　　　The inside viewed from the bar area.

(Photo captions)
Top / The service wagon and table setting.
Middle / The wine cellar as a wall design.
Bottom / THe gift shop at the lobby level.

ウエット バー（Wet bar)のあるホスピタリティ スイートルームのパーラー

ベッドルーム

(Photo captions – page 12)
Top / The hospitality suite room having a wet bar.
Bottom / The bedroom.

(Photo captions – page 13)
Top / "The View Restaurant" (196 seats) and the lounge (505 seats)
   are open at the 46th to 48th floors.
   The floors above the 9th are provided with exclusive elevators.
Left, bottom / The parlor viewed from Wet bar.
Right, bottom / The rotary restaurant on the roof featuring the brass
   finish.

"The View Restaurant"(196席)とラウンジ(505席)が46〜48階にあり　9階より専用エレベーターがある

ウエット バーよりパーラーをみる

ブラスを配した回転式屋上レストラン

13

29,025sq.-ftの大宴会場　10のセクションに分けることができ　最大3500名を収容できる
The large banquet hall, 29,025 sq. ft.; divided into 10 sections, it can accommodate 3,500 guests at maximum.

17階建吹抜けアトリウム　Jhon C.Portman の設計で自ら経営者でもある
The atrium with a stairwell through 17 stories. Designed by John C. Portman who is also owner.

THE PORTMAN
SAN FRANCISCO

500 Post Street San Francisco, CA 94102
Phone/415-771-8600

得意のシースルー エレヘーター
The see-through elevator — one of the hotel's boastful features.

メインロビーのある3階フロアより天窓を配したアトリウムをみる　　　　　　The atrium with a skylight viewed from the 3rd floor where the main lobby lies.

グラス製の雨除けを設置した外観

ブリックとコンクリートで構成した外観全景

エレベーター内よりフロントデスクをみる

3階ロビーのエレベーターホール　　The elevator hall at the 3rd floor lobby.

入口ドアとドアマン

パーソナル バーレー サービス（Personal Valet Service）
のユニークなコンセプトがこのホテルの特徴　24時
間待機のシステム

アーチ状の照明を配した3階のレセプション

(Photo captions — page 16)
Left, bottom / The appearance with a glass
　　protection against rain.
Right, bottom / The entire appearance consist-
　　ing of bricks and concrete.

(Photo captions — page 17)
From above:
● The front desk viewed from inside the eleva-
　tor.
● The entrance door and doorman.
● The unique concept "personal valet service"
　is one of the main features of this hotel.
Left, bottom / The 3rd floor reception where
　　arched lighting is provided.

最上階にある"The Club"宿泊客専用のサロンでコンチネンタルブレックファースト　カクテル　ティーなどを提供している

"The Club" at the highest floor — a salon exclusive for stayers who are served a cup of continental breakfast cocktail tea.

"The Club"にあるバーのサービスエリア
The service area of a bar within "The Club."

3階にある"The Bar"の入口
The entrance to "The Bar" at the 3rd floor.

ゆったりとした"The Bar"のラウンジ カクテルやリフレッシュメントを提供する　The spacious lounge of "The Bar" — cocktails, refreshments, etc. are served.

"The Grill"（100席）唯一のメインダイニングて朝食　ランチ　ディナーを提供する
"The Grill" (100 seats) – the only main dining where breakfast, lunch and dinner are served.

シェフのFred Halpert 氏と料理
Chef, Mr. Fred Halpert, and his dishes.

テーブルセッティング　　　　　　　　　　　　The table setting.

ピアノ越しに"The Bar"をみる

"The Bar" viewed from across the piano.

2階の大宴会場"Olympic Ballroom"

"Olympic Ballroom" — a large banquet hall at the 2nd floor.

3階ロビーレベルより宴会及び会議室へ通じる階段

The staircase leading from the 3rd floor lobby level to the banquet hall and conference rooms.

ホテル自慢の"Executive Conference Center"のコンシアージ サービス エリア
The concierge service area at the "Executive Conference Center" – one of the boastful features of this hotel.

オーディオ ビジュアル装置付きの会議室（4室）
One of the four conference rooms equipped with audiovisual units.

ビュッフェ ダイニングルームが中央に併設され会議と食事が同じ場所でできる

ザ ポートマン サンフランシスコ

現代ホテル建築 特にユニークで広大なアトリウムを採り入れた設計 デザインで有名な建築家John C.Portmanが初めて自分の名を冠したホテルをオープンした。これまでのデザイン指向からサービス指向へと転換を試み従来のアトリウムやグラス エレベーターといった特長は残しながらも 建築デザインそのものをサービス中心に考えて建てたホテルとしている。たとえば ほぼ四角形の建物の三辺に客室を配し 残りの一辺はサービス用スペースとなっている。各階に24時間待機のパーソナル バレーサービスをこの部分に置き 客の到着時のティー サービス 荷ほどき 入浴の準備 プレス 靴磨き 新聞の配達 外出の都度部屋の掃除といったあらゆる要望に応えている。 Portman 氏自身の経験から アジアにおけるサービスを高く評価し このホテルをオープンするに当たって「ペニンシュラグループ オブ ホテルズ(ホンコン)」と提携して これらのサービスのノウハウを学ぶといった新しいホテル コンセプトを はじめて米国に導入した話題のホテルである。

デベロッパー/Portman Properties, Atlanta
設計/Jhon Portman & Associates, Inc. Atlanta
オープン/1987年 9 月17日
規模・客室数/21階建 348室(内ペニンシュラ スイート 16室)
その他の施設/ノン スモーキングフロアー(13・14階) 身体障害者用部屋(11室) エクゼクティブ コンフェレンス センター
投資額/ 1 億ドル

THE PORTMAN San Francisco

An architect well-known for his modern hotel design incorporating, among others, a unique, extensive atrium, Mr. John C. Portman inaugurated the first of "Portman" hotels.
With the aim to change from the conventional design type to the service type, this hotel has been built with an emphasis on services, while employing conventional design features, such as atrium and glassed elevators. For instance, guest rooms are arranged along three sides of the nearly square building, and the remaining side is used as a service space. At the side of each floor a 24-hour on-the-alert personal valet service is offered, complying thus with any requests, from tea service at the time of guest arrival to unpacking, preparation of the bath, ironing, shoe polishing, newspaper delivery, cleaning the room whenever the guests are absent, etc. In light of his experiences, Mr. Portman rated highly services in Asia. Thus, in opening this hotel bearing his own name, he tied up with "Peninsula Group of Hotels (Peninsula–Hong Kong)," learning about the knowhow of those services, introducing a new hotel concept, thus drawing hot attention.

500 Post Street, San Francisco, CA 94102
Phone: 415-771-8600

Developer / Portman Properties, Atlanta
Design / John Portman & Associates, Inc., Atlanta
Opened / September 17, 1987
Scale, number of guest rooms / 21 stories, 348 rooms (incl. 16 peninsular suite rooms)
Other facilities / Non-smoking floors (13th and 14th), rooms (11) for the physically handicapped, executive conference center.
Investment / $100 million

The buffet is open beside the dining room in the center, so that you can hold a conference and have a meal at the same place.

3/ウェット バーの付いたスペシャル スイートのダイニング

1/高価な調度品を備えたスペシャル スイート ルームのリビング

2/ブラスのボールを使用したマスターズ ヘッドルーム

4/マホガニーのコンソールを備えたスイート ルーム

5/全面大理石を使用したバスルーム

6/洗面台には小型のテレビまである

7/バスタブ廻り

(Photo captions)

1/ The special suite room's living room equipped with expensive furniture.

2/ Master's bedroom using a brass ball.

3/ The dining with a wet bar.

4/ The suite room equipped with a mahogany console.

5/ The bathroom using marble over the entire surface.

6/ The washstand is equipped even with a small TV set.

7/ Around the bathtub.

ヨーロッパ調ホテルの外観（30階建322室）　　　　　　The appearance of the European style hotel.

ℂENTURY·PLAZA
TOWER

2055 Avenue of the stars Los Angeles, CA 90067
Phone/213-277-2000

手前は"Centtury plaza Hotel"の旧館　　Old "Century Plaza Hotel" in your side.

円形に張り出したドライブ ウェイ エントランス
The driveway entrance projected circularly.

車の Valet Service 専用コーナー
The special car valet service corner.

エントランスの天井デザイン　The entrance's ceiling design.

レセプション廻り　エクレクティックなインテリアデザインを展開している

タワー専用のフロント デスク

格調あるエントランスホール　　　　The entrance hall having a dignified atmosphere.

レセプション近くのギフトショップ　　　　The gift shop near the reception.

(Photo captions)
Middle, top / The reception area where an eclectic interior design is arranged.
Middle, bottom / The front desk exclusive for the tower.

ロビー階奥の庭園に面したガーデン レストラン "The Terrace"

"The Terrace" の入口廻り

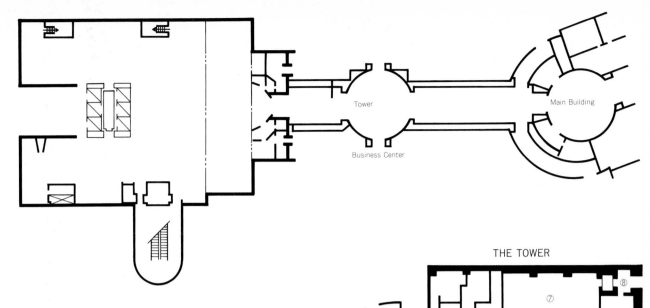

Tower

Business Center

Main Building

センチュリー プラザ タワー

アメリカのホテルの中でも最高級のプレステージを誇るホテルの一つ「CENTURY PLAZA」(750室) がオープンしたのが1966年6月1日であった。日系建築家ミノル山崎氏の設計によるエレガントなデザインは高く評価されている。

そして1984年の暮に隣接して30階建てのタワー(322室) を完成した。タワー完成時の最初のオフィシャル ゲストはレーガン大統領夫妻であった。最上階のPlaza Suiteは8,600 sq,-ft. の広さで これは世界のホテルの中でも最も広く 高価なスィートルームである。各フロアを14室に制限したデラックスな客室は 東洋と西洋を織り混ぜたインテリアで構成している。また美術館を想像させる絵画やアンティークの置物や備品などのコレクションだけでも約100万ドルを投じている。本館とタワーを結ぶコンコースはまるでギャラリーである。

新しく2つのレストランと2つのバーラウンジがタワーに加わった。

オーナー・デベロッパー/Century City, Inc.

経営/Westin Hotel and Resorts, Seattle

設計/建築・Skidmore, Owings and Merrill, San Francisco
　　　内装 & 企画・Intradesign, Inc. Los Angeles

オープン/1984年12月27日

規模・客室数/30階建322室

投資額/8,500万ドル

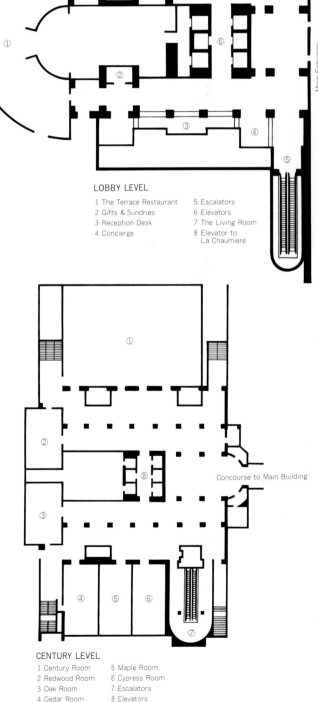

THE TOWER

LOBBY LEVEL

1 .The Terrace Restaurant	5 .Escalators
2 .Gifts & Sundries	6 .Elevators
3 .Reception Desk	7 .The Living Room
4 .Concierge	8 .Elevator to La Chaumiere

Main Entrance

Concourse to Main Building

CENTURY LEVEL

1 .Century Room	5 .Maple Room
2 .Redwood Room	6 .Cypress Room
3 .Oak Room	7 .Escalators
4 .Cedar Room	8 .Elevators

CENTURY PLAZA TOWER

It was June 1, 1966, that "Century Plaza," one of the most prestigious hotels in the U.S. opened. Having 750 rooms, and elegantly designed by Mr. Minoru Yamazaki, a Japanese architect, this hotel is highly rated.

Towards the end of 1984, adjacent to it, a 30-storied tower (having 322 rooms) was completed. The first official guests at the time of completion were President Reagan and his wife. Plaza Suite at the highest floor is 8,000 square feet — widest, and it is the most expensive suite room in the world.

The number of guest rooms at each floor is limited to 14. These deluxe guest rooms feature an interior mixing-up Oriental and Western elements. About one million dollars have been invested in a collection of paintings and antique ornaments and fixtures which remind us of an art museum. The concourse connecting the main building and the tower looks like a gallery.

Two restaurants and two bar lounges have been added recently to the tower.

2055 Avenue of the Stars, Los Angeles, CA 90067
Phone: 213-277-2000

Owner · developer / Century City, Inc.
Management / Westin Hotel and Resorts, Seattle
Design / Architecture: Skidmore, Owings and Merrill, San Francisco
　　　Interior & plan: Intradesign, Inc., Los Angeles
Opened / December 27, 1984
Scale, number of guest rooms / 30 stories, 322 rooms
Investment / $85 million

テラス風ダイニングルームを加えた高級レストラン"La Chaumiere"（114席）
"La Chaumiere" (114 seats) – a high-class restaurant combined with a terrace-like dining room.

"La Chaumiere Bar"のラウンジ
The lounge of "La Chaumiere Bar."

古典絵画が飾られているバーカウンター
The bar counter decorated with classic paintings.

スタイリッシュなリビングルームを持つ"The Living Room"のバーラウンジ　The bar lounge of "The Living Room" having a stylish living room.

オリエンタル風なバーカウンター
The bar counter in an Oriental style.

ロビーの右手にある"The Living Room"
"The Living Room" in the right side of the lobby.

プレジデンシャル スイート ルームの格調あるリビング ルーム
The dignified living room of presidential suite room.

電話やテレビのリモートコントロール
Remote controlling the phone or TV.

ライティング デスク
The writing desk.

バスルームのアメニティ
The bathroom's amenities.

カノピー ヘッド
The canopy bed.

ミニ ウェット バー
The mini wet bar.

スイート ルームのエレガントな雰囲気を醸しだすベッド ルーム　　　The bedroom of a suite room giving an elegant atmosphere.

リビングルーム　　　The living room.

各部屋にはシャワールームが備えてある
Each guest room is provided with a shower room.

テーブル　セッティング

タワーと旧館を結ぶコンコース

ロビーレベルとコンコースレベルに通じるエスカレーターホール

(Photo captions)
Top / The table setting.
Middle / The concourse linking the tower with the old building.
Bottom / The escalator hall leading to the lobby level and concourse level.

6,000 sq.-ft.　800人収容の宴会場"Century Room"
The "Century Room" – a banquet hall (6,000 sq. ft. wide), capable of accommodating 800 persons.

大理石の柱がある宴会場のロビー　　The lobby of the banquet hall with marble columns.

シカゴ リバーに沿って建つホテルの外観（別名とうもろこしビル） The appearance of the hotel standing along River Chicago.

hotel nikko chicago

320 North Dearborn Street Chicago, Ⅰ Ⅰ inois 60610
Phone/312-744-1900

正面外観をみる The front appearance.

"The Hana Lounge"（100席）のバーカウンター

The bar counter of "The Hana Lounge" (100 seats).

"The Hana Lounge"は日本庭園に面している

"The Hana Lounge" is facing the Japanese garden.

近代的な装置を備えたフロント オフィス

The front office with modern equipment.

ロビー脇の公衆電話ブース
The public telephone booth beside the lobby.

LES CELEBRITES(1st Floor)

Kitchen

Main Dining Room

Private Room

Main Dining Room

SYC Area

Bar

Main Dining Room

Lounge

Overflow Sealing

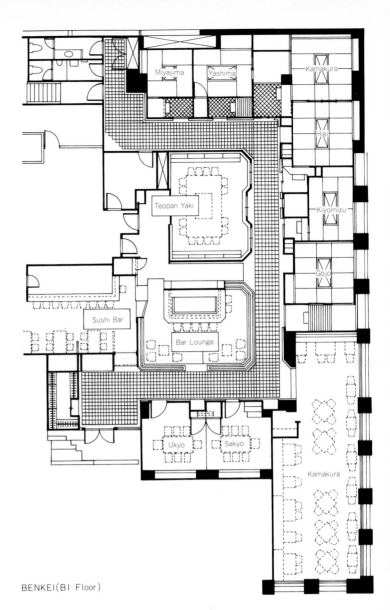

Miyajima Yashima Kamakura

Hiei

Teppan Yaki

Kiyomizu

Gojo

Sushi Bar

Bar Lounge

Ukyo Sakyo

Kamakura

BENKEI(BI Floor)

ホテル ニッコー シカゴ

日本航空の関連会社である「㈱日本航空開発」は 国内外にネットワーク
を広げ 1987年9月1日現在22ホテル 8801室を運営するワールドワイ
ドなホテルとして発展を続けている。最近では北アメリカのニューヨー
ク サンフランシスコ シカゴとメキシコシティなど大都市に進出を果
した。1987年10月1日 シカゴ川に面し 同市の名物ビル「マリナ シテ
ィ」に隣接「マーチャンダイズマート」にも近い好立地にオープンした。
同ホテルはアメリカ有数の総合建築会社であるティッシュマン リアルテ
ィ & コンストラクション社（Tishman Realty & Construction Co.,
Inc.)とのジョイントベンチャー事業で 地上20階 客室数425室の規模で
ある。50万ドルを越える東洋や現代の芸術作品をはじめ あちこちに東
西の文化を感じさせるインテリアが導入されている。和食レストランも
あって寿司や会席料理も味わえ 7年ぶりの大型ホテルの開業とあって
地元シカゴでは話題となっている。

設計・施工/Tishman Realty & Co.,Inc.
設計・建築・Hellmuth, Obata & Kassabaum, Inc. St Louis
　　内装・Hirsh/Bendner and Associates, Santa Monica
オープン/1987年10月1日
規模・客室数/地上20階 地下3階建(422,000 sq.-ft) 425室
料飲施設/3：レ・セレブリテ(レストラン & バー)195席 弁慶(和食レス
　　トラン)150席 ハナラウンジ(ラウンジ)100席
宴会・会議場/大宴会場1室 コンファレンスルーム4室 ミーティング
　　ルーム14室
その他の施設/ビジネスセンター ヘルスクラブ

HOTEL NIKKO CHICAGO

Japan Air Line Development Co., an affiliate of Japan Air Line Co.,
has expanded steadily its networks in Japan and overseas. As of
September 1, 1987, it is operating 22 hotels (with 8,801 rooms),
which allows it to develop itself into a worldwide hotel chain.
Recently, its network has advanced into large cities of North America,
such as New York, San Francisco, Chicago and Mexico City. On
October 1, 1987, facing River Chicago and adjacent to "Marina City,"
while being also near the "Merchandising Mart," this hotel has been
opened at the ideal location. Built in a joint venture with Tishman
Realty & Construction Co., Inc., this hotel features 20 stories above
the ground, with 425 guest rooms. Eastern and modern art works
valued at more than $500,000 are arranged here and there, and
the interior reminds us of Eastern and Western culture. A Japanese
dish restaurant is also provided, serving 'sushi' and 'kaiseki.'
As a large hotel opened after 7 years, it is drawing much attention
from the Chicago's public.

320 North Dearborn Street, Chicago, Illinois 60610
Phone: 312-744-1900

Design, installation / Tishman Realty & Construction Co.
Design / Architecture: Hellmuth, Obata & Kassabaum, Inc., St. Louis
　　Interior: Hirsh/Bendner and Associates, Santa Monica
Opened / October 1, 1987
Scale, number of guest rooms / 20 stories above and
　　3 under the ground (422,000 sq. ft.), 425 rooms
Eating/drinking facilities / Les Celebrites (restaurant & bar, 195 seats),
　　Benkay (Japanese dish restaurant, 100 seats),
　　Hana (lounge, 100 seats)
Banquet hall, boardroom and other facilities / Large banquet hall (1),
　　conference rooms (4), meeting rooms (14), health club, business
　　center.

レストラン"Les Celebrites"のファサード（ロビーレベル）
The facade (lobby level) of the restaurant "Les Celebrites."

"Les Celebrites"のバーコーナー　　　The bar corner of "Les Celebrites."

バーよりレストラン方向をみる　　　The restaurant viewed from the bar.

コンテンポラリー アメリカン レストランの"Les Celebrites"（100席）はシカゴ リバーに面している
The contemporary American restaurant "Les Celebrites" (100 seats) is facing River Chicago.

8,400sq.-ft.の"ニッコー グランド ボールルーム"3室に分けることもできる　8,400 sq. ft. "Nikko Grand Ballroom" – may be partitioned into three rooms.

"エグゼクティブ ボードルーム"のゆったりした会議室

The "Executive Boardroom" – a spacious conference room.

ビュッフェ パーティーがセットされた宴会場
The banquet hall where a buffet party has been set.

18〜20階を占める"ニッコー フロア"の専用ラウンジ
The lounge exclusive for "Nikko Floor" that occupies the 18th to 20th floors.

日本料理 "Benkey" (150席)
The Japanese dish restaurant "Benkey" (150 seats).

寿司バーのカウンター席　'Sushi' bar's counter.

シカゴ リバーに面した "Benkey" のメインダイニングルーム　この他に鉄板焼コーナー　和室がある

"Benkey" の中央部にあるバーコーナー

The bar corner in the center of "Benkey."

Top / The main dining room of "Benkey." facing River Chicago. The hot plate dish corner and Japanese room are also available.

標準的客室の調度類
The furniture and utensils of a standard guest room.

クインサイズのベッドルーム　　The queen-size bedroom.

プレジデンシャル スイートのベッドルーム
The bedroom of a presidential suite room.

サウナ室が付いたスイートルームのバスルーム
The bathroom of a suite room provided with a sauna room.

スイートルームのリビングルーム　　The living room of a suite room.

スイートルームに併設するダイニングルーム　　The dining room installed in a suite room.

オリエンタル調とコンテンポラリーなデザインのもう1つのスイートのヘッドルーム
Another suite bedroom featuring the Oriental and contemporary patterns of design.

マスターベッドルーム
The master bedroom.

スイートのリビングルーム
The living room of a suite room.

大理石のバスルーム　The marbled bathroom.

クリーク(入江)に沿って建つグラスウォールのホテル(14階)　The glass-walled hotel (14-storied) standing along the creek.

エンターテイメント ラウンジの入口は別になっている
The entertainment lounge's entrance is separately provided.

左に宴会場建物が付帯するホテルのファサード
The hotel's facade to whose left side is attached the banquet hall building.

THE WESTIN CYPRESS CREEK

400 Corporate Drive Fort Lauderdale, Florida 33334
Phone/305-772-1331

ロビーとレセプション　　The lobby and reception.

ロビーより大宴会場へ続く通路
The passage leading from the lobby to the large banquet hall.

"The Fountain Cafe"（172席）カジュアルレストランとしてビュッフェ コーナーを設けている

クリークに突き出した形のプール　軽食や飲物のサービス施設もある
The pool projected to the creek. Snack and drinks service facilities are also available.

"The Fountain Cafe" (172 seats) — as a casual restaurant, a buffet corner is provided.

"The Fountain Cafe"の入口廻り
Around the entrance to "The Fountain Cafe."

"The Lakeside Pavilion"のラウンジ
The lounge of "The Lake-side Pavilion."

ロビーよりレストラン バーに通じるパブリックスペース
The public space leading to the restaurant bar from the lobby.

ランチタイムのビュッフェと料理   The buffet at lunch time.

上・下/客室のデザインはモダンとクラッシックの調和がよくとれている

Top, bottom / The guest room design features a harmony between modern and classic elements.

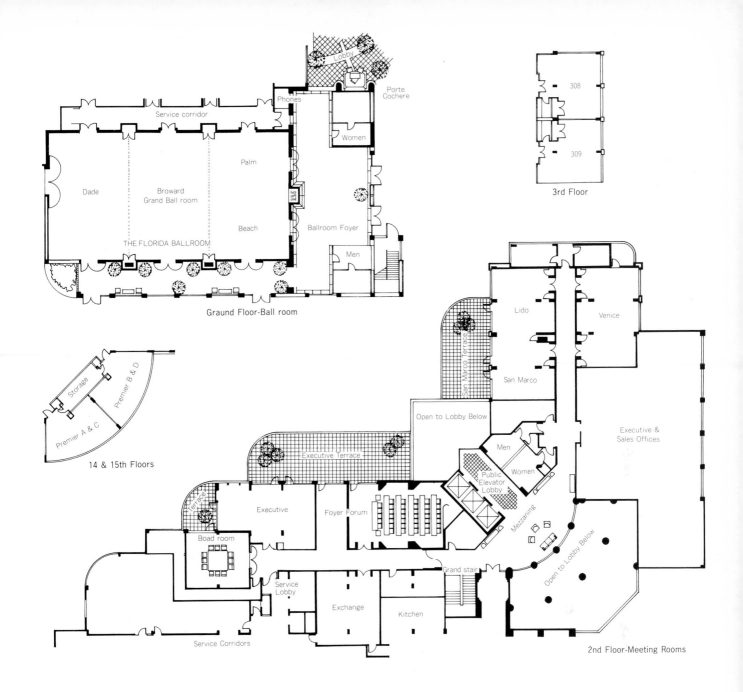

Lobby
Porte Cochere
Phones
Service corridor
Women
Palm
Dade
Broward Grand Ball room
Beach
THE FLORIDA BALLROOM
Ballroom Foyer
Men
Graund Floor-Ball room

3rd Floor
308
309

Storage
Premier B & D
Premier A & C
14 & 15th Floors

Lido
Venice
San Marco Terrace
San Marco
Open to Lobby Below
Executive & Sales Offices
Executive Terrace
Men
Public Elevator Lobby
Women
Terrace
Executive
Foyer Forum
Mezzanine
Board room
Open to Lobby Below
Service Lobby
Grand stair
Exchange
Kitchen
Service Corridors
2nd Floor-Meeting Rooms

ザ ウエスティン サイプレス クリーク

「ウエスティン ホテル」がフロリダ州に進出した最初のホテルである。
この南フロリダのフォート ローダーデイル地域は　マイアミと並んで高
級別荘地としても有名であるが　その一方でアメリカ第２のコンピュー
ター産業が盛んな所で　研究所やオフィスが多い所でもある。それらに
関係するビジネス客を対象にしてオフィス センターの中に建てられ　17
室の会議室をはじめトータルで15,300 sq,-ft. の宴会及び会議室を設けて
いる。客室のテーブルは大きめのものを備え付けたり２フロアはノンス
モーキング客専用のフロアとするなどの配慮もある。また　ヘルスクラ
ブやジョギングコース　プールといった健康指向の設備　エンターテイ
メント ラウンジといったナイトスポットを設けるなど　ビジネスとレジ
ャーを上手にかけ合わせた近代的なホテルライフを提供している。

オープン/1987年１月
規標・客室数/地上14階建　294室(内スイート 33室)
料飲施設/Cypress Room(レストラン)70席　Fountain Cafe(カフェ＆レ
　　　　　ストラン)172席　Peppers(ダンス＆カクテル)192席 Lakeside
　　　　　Pavillon, Pool-side(ラウンジ)
宴会・会議場/会議室17室(15,300sq.-ft.)
その他の施設/ヘルスクラブ(サウナ付)ジョギングコース 温水プール(屋
　　　　　外)

THE WESTIN CYPRESS CREEK

The first hotel opened in Florida by "Westin Hotel." Fort Lauderdale, South Florida, like Miami, is famous as a high class residential quarter. It is also the 2nd most important center of the computer industry, and it is equipped with many research institutes and offices. Intended for guests imvolved in business, this hotel has been built within the office center. There are conference rooms (17) and banquet halls, covering an area of 15,300 sq. ft. Each guest room is provided with a large table, and two floors are used exclusively for non-smoking guests. Health-oriented facilities (a health club, jogging course, pool, etc.), and night spots (entertainment lounge, etc.) are also provided to offer to the guests a modern hotel life by combining skillfully business and leisure activities.

400 Corporate Drive, Fort Lauderdale, Florida 33334
Phone: 305-772-1331

Opened / January 1, 1987
Scale, number of guest rooms / 14 stories, 294 rooms
　　(incl. 33 suite rooms)
Eating/drinking facilities / Cypress room (restaurant, 70 seats),
　　Fountain cafe (cafe & restaurant, 172 seats),
　　Peppers (dance & cocktail, 192 seats),
　　Lake-side pavilion, Pool-side (lounge)
Banquet hall, boardroom / Boardrooms (17) (15,300 sq. ft.)
Other facilities / Health club (with a sauna),
　　jogging course, hot water pool (outdoors)

メインダイニング"The Cypress Room"のエントランスホール
The entrance hall of the main dining "The Cypress Room."

"The Cypress Room"(70席)はゴールドメダルに輝く数々の料理を提供している
"The Cypress Room" (70 seats) serves a variety of dishes which have been awarded gold medals.

落ち着きのあるバーエリア　The bar area with a composed mood.

ワインボトルをディスプレイしたプライベートルーム
A private room where wine bottles are displayed.

最上階の"エグゼクティブ クラブ"のラウンジ
The lounge of "Executive Club" at the highest floor.

50

エンターテイメント ラウンジ"Pepper's"（192席）のバーカウンター
The bar counter of the entertainment lounge "Pepper's" (192 seats).

オーディオ ビジュアル機器をフルにいかしたナイトスポット
The night spot where audiovisual units are fully utilized.

モダン クラッシック調のレセプション

The reception in a modern plus classic style.

ドライブウエイとエントランス エリア
The driveway and entrance area.

KANSAS CITY
Marriott®
PLAZA

4445 Main Street Kansas City, Missouri 64111
Phone/816-531-3000

18階建て　296室の客室をもつ外観
The appearance of the 18-storied hotel having 296 seats.

1階のロビーとピアノバー
The lobby and piano bar at the 1st floor.

ピアノバーのカウンター廻り

ゆったりと席をとった"Curios"の店内

"Curios"のエントランス廻り

フルサービスのレストラン"Curios"(158席)の窓側客席
The window-side guest seats of the full-service restaurant "Curios" (158 seats).

(Photo captions)
Top / Around the piano bar's counter.
Middle / Inside "Curios" where guest seats are
    spaciously arranged.
Bottom / Around the entrance to "Curios."

カンサス シティ マリオット プラザ

おそらくアメリカ中で一番古いショッピング センターの発祥地として
「The Country Club Plaza」が当地カンサスシティにある。ダウンタウ
ンより5分の距離で スペイン情緒のある街としても有名。ショップや
レストラン ギャラリー エンターテイメントプレイスなどが150店以
上集まって構成されている。ここを中心にして周囲に8つのホテルが建
ち コンベンションやレジャー客に応えている。
この「マリオット プラザホテル」は客室数296室という中規模のシティホ
テルであるが 大宴会場の他に18の会議室を備えていながら レストラ
ンは1ヵ所のみ。これは会議室でも食事ができるように計画されている
からだ。また エンターテイメント ラウンジ内にビュッフェを設けてデ
イタイムのグループ客に開放したり 夜は魅力のあるオードブルを中心
としたビュッフェをサービスしている。今はやりのヘルスクラブやプー
ルなども備え 最大限有効的に運営されているホテルの一例でもある。
経営者/Outlook Partners Kansas City
オープン/1987年3月
規模・客室数/地上18階建(218,000 sq,-ft) 296室(内スイート18室)
料飲施設/3：Curios(フルサービスレストラン)158席 Isla-The Club(エ
　　　　ンターテイメントラウンジ)598席 The Casual piano bar(バ
　　　　ー)
宴会場・会議場/大宴会場(5,628sq,-ft.) 会議室18室(15,000sq,-ft.)
その他の施設/ヘルスクラブ(屋内プール付)

客室へ通じるエレベーターホール　The elevator hall leading to guest rooms.

Kansas City MARRIOTT PLAZA

"The Country Club Plaza," which is probably the oldest shopping
center in America, is located in Kansas City. Five minutes by car from
the downtown, and it is famous as a city with a Spanish atmosphere.
It consists of more than 150 shops, restaurants, galleries, entertainment places. Eight hotels are surrounding this hotel, to satisfy the
needs of convention and leisure guests.
This "Marriott Plaza" is a medium-size city hotel with 296 guest
rooms. In addition to a large banquet hall, there are 18 conference
rooms, but with only one restaurant. This is due to the fact that
meals are served in conference rooms. A buffet is provided in the
entertainment lounge, and it is opened to groups of guests during
daytime. At night, a buffet is served to guests with delicious hors
d'œuvre. This installation is also provided with a health club, a pool,
etc. which are currently popular, and is operated most effectively.

4445 Main Street, Kansas City, Missouri 64111
Phone: 816-531-3000

Owner / Outlook Partners Kansas City
Opened / March 1987
Scale, number of guest rooms / 18 stories (218,000 sq. ft.),
　　296 rooms (incl. 18 suite rooms)
Eating/drinking facilities / Curios (full-service restaurant, 158 seats),
　　Isla-The Club (entertainment lounge, 598 seats),
　　The casual piano bar (bar)
Banquet hall, boardroom / Large banquet hall (5,628 sq. ft.),
　　Boardrooms (18) (15,000 sq. ft.)
Other facilities / Health club (with an indoor pool),
　　Parking (accommodating 210 cars)
Total investment / $32 million

1階ロビーと2階会議室　レストランを結ぶ階段
The staircase connecting the 1st floor lobby with the boardroom and
restaurant at the 2nd floor.

At the lounge with concierge, you can take breakfast or cocktail, or can
be checked in/out.

コンシアージ レベルのラウンジは朝食やカクテルの他チェックイン アウトもできる

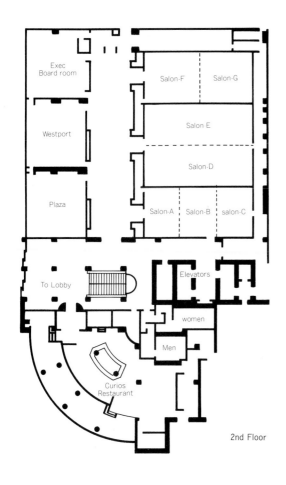

ヘルスクラブのプール　　　The health club's pool.

Exec Board room

Salon-F | Salon-G

Westport

Salon E

Salon-D

Plaza

Salon-A | Salon-B | salon-C

To Lobby

Elevators

women

Men

Curios Restaurant

2nd Floor

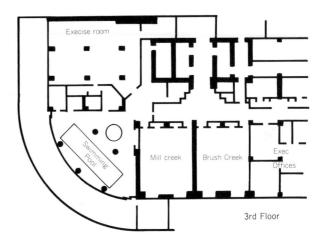

Execise room

Swimming Pool

Mill creek | Brush Creek | Exec Offices

3rd Floor

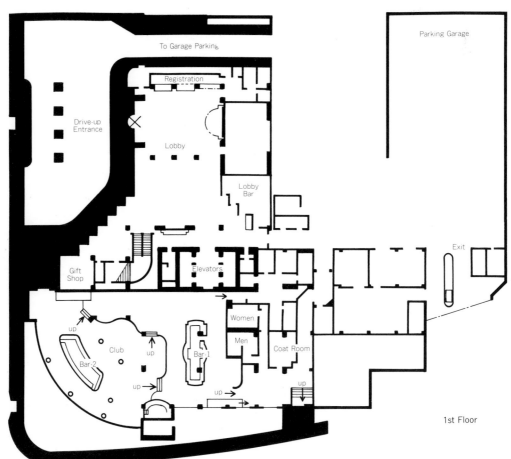

Parking Garage

To Garage Parking

Registration

Drive-up Entrance

Lobby

Lobby Bar

Exit

Gift Shop

Elevators

Women

Men | Coat Room

up

Club

up

Bar-1

up

Bar-2

up

up

1st Floor

55

エンターテイメント ラウンジの"Isla"(598席)には 2つのバーカウンターを中心にダンスフロアとラウンジがある
At the entertainment lounge "Isla" (598 seats), there are a dance floor and lounge, with two bar counters in the center.

専用の入口　　　　　　The exclusive entrance.

ファンタジックなラウンジのコーナー　　　The fantastic lounge corner.

"Isla"とはスペイン語で"島"という意味　夜のオアシスでもある

"Isla" means an "island" in Spanish. It may be said to be a night oasis.

月曜から金曜まで〈Hungry Hour Buffet〉（PM5：00〜8：00）が提供される

"Hungry Hour Buffet" (5:00 p.m. to 8:00 p.m.) is served from Monday till Friday.

入口よりラウンジの奥をみる

Looking into the inner part of the lounge from the entrance.

上・下／プレジデンシャル スイート ルームのリビングルームとベッドルーム及びレギュラー ルームのバスルーム

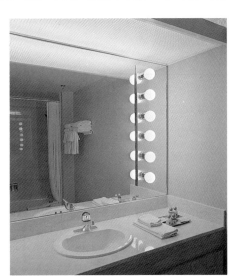

Top-Bottom/The living room and bedroom of a presidential suite room, and the bathroom of a regular room.

サンフランシスコのショッピング エリア"ユニオン スクウェア"に程近いマーケットストリートよりみた外観
The hotel's appearance viewed from the market street close to San Francisco's shopping area "Union Square."

エントランス廻り　　　　　　　　　　Around the entrance.

レンタカーのカウンター　　　The rent-a-car counter.

２階レストラン フロアのロビーラウンジ "Piazza" ３〜４階のバンケット フロアまで吹抜け
The lobby lounge "Piazza" at the restaurant floor (2nd floor), with the stairwell up to the 3rd/4th banquet floors.

１〜４階までを結ぶ階段
The staircase connecting the 1st to 4th floors.

1015室のレセプション
The reception at the room 1015.

ホテルの出入口
The hotel's entrance/exit.

カジュアルレストラン"Veranda"のダイニングルーム

パスタサラダが中心のビュッフェコーナーとシェフの John Marshall

"ルネッサンス クラブ ラウンジ"では 朝食やカクテルと共にフリー オードブルが提供される

"Veranda"（200席）は 彫像や大理石の泉を配してある
"Veranda" (200 seats) comes with statues, a marbled fountain, etc.

"ルネッサンス クラブ ラウンジ"（31階）は 専任のコンシアージが客の応対をしてくれる
At "Renaissance Club Lounge" (31-storied), full-time concierges are receiving guests.

(Photo captions)
Top / The dining room of the casual restaurant "Veranda."
Middle / The buffet corner mainly serving pasta salads, and the chef, John Marshall.
Bottom / At "Renaissance Club Lounge" you are served breakfast, cocktail and free hors d'œuvre.

ラマダ ルネッサンス ホテル

全世界に650以上のホテルを展開するラマダホテル グループが新しいコンセプトのホテルを「ルネッサンス」というネーミングで展開している。1988年までには50ヵ所以上に増える計画である。従来に比べより良いサービスと施設 アメニティなどを備え 法外なコストではなく 安心して泊まれるホテルというのが主なコンセプトのねらいである。
1億3,000万ドルを投じ 地上32階 客室数1,015室を有するこのホテルから 次のような興味深い数字を幾つかひろってみた。ベッド数1,500 ランプの数2,440 カーペットの長さのトータル 54,360ヤード 大理石240トン 3,624の窓枠パネル……などが使用されている。また 55,000食以上が毎月調理される予定で これらは2つのレストランとルームサービス 従業員食堂を含む数字である。さらに専任のアートコンサルタントが収集した絵画や彫刻を含む装飾品に100万ドル以上を投じ 名実共にラマダホテルチェーンのフラッグシップホテルとして位置づけられている。

経営者/International Hoteliers Ltd.
設計/建築・Daniel Mann, Johnson & Mendenhall, San Francisco
　　　　　DMJM/Curtis and Davis, New Orleans
　　　内装・Hirsch/Bedner & Associates, Santa Monica
施工/Swinerton & Walberg Co., San Francisco
オープン/1984年11月15日
規模・客室数/地上32階建(800,000sq,-ft.) 1,015室
料飲施設/4：Piazza Lobby Lounge(ラウンジ)130席　Allegro cocktail
　　　　Lounge(ラウンジ)65席　Veranda Restaurant(レストラン)200
　　　　席　Corintia Restaurant(レストラン)65席
宴会・会議場/大宴会場(17,500sq.-ft. ルネッサンスBallroom と Junior
　　　　Ballroomを含む)　会議室17室　エグゼクティブ ボードルーム3室
その他の施設/ヘルスクラブ　ギフトショップ

RAMADA RENAISSANCE HOTEL

Ramadas Group, which is operating more than 650 hotels across the world, is developing new-concept hotels using the name of "Renaissance." It is expected that within 1988 these new-concept hotels will be opened at more than 50 locations. The new concept has the aim to provide guests with services, facilities, amenities, etc. better than those offered by conventional hotels, with reasonable prices, ensuring thus a quiet stay.
The 32-storied hotel, for which 130 million dollars have been invested, is provided with 1,015 guest rooms. Concerning this hotel, interesting figures are known, such as – number of beds – 1,500, number of lamps – 2,440, total length of carpet – 54,360 yards, quantity of marble – 240 tons, number of window frame panels – 3,624. Also, more than 55,000 meals are prepared every month, including those served in both restaurants, those for room services and those in the employees' dining hall.
With more than one million dollars invested in ornaments, including paintings and sculptures collected by a full-time art consultant, this hotel can be considered as the flagship hotel of Ramadas hotel chain in both name and reality.

55 Cyrill Maglin Street, San Francisco, CA 94102
Phone: 415-392-8000

Owner / International Hoteliers Ltd.
Design / Architecture: Daniel, Mann, Johnson & Mendenhall, San Francisco
　　DMJM/Curtis and Davis, New Orleans
　　Interior: Hirsch/Bedner & Associates, Santa Monica
Installation / Swinerton & Walberg Co., San Francisco
Opened / November 15, 1984
Scale, number of guest rooms / 32 stories (800,000 sq. ft.),
　　1,015 rooms
Eating/drinking facilities / Piazza lobby lounge (lounge, 130 seats),
　　Allegro cocktail lounge (lounge, 65 seats),
　　Veranda restaurant (restaurant, 200 seats),
　　Corintia restaurant (restaurant, 65 seats)
Banquet hall, boardroom / Boardrooms (17),
　　Large banquet hall (17,500 sq. ft., incl. Renaissance ballroom and junior ballroom), Executive boardrooms (3)
Other facilities / Health club, Gift shop,
　　Parking (capable of accommodating 150 cars)

1階エントランスホール　左がレストランフロアの階段　正面奥にフロントレセプション
The 1st floor entrance hall – in the left is the staircase leading to the restaurant floor. At a front inner part is visible the front reception.

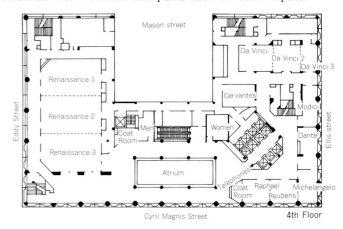

4th Floor

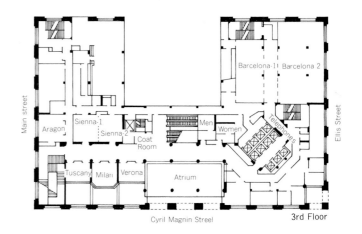

3rd Floor

バンケット フロアより"Piazza"のロビーラウンジをみる
The lobby lounge "Piazza" viewed from the banquet floor.

2階のギフトショップ
The gift shop at the 2nd floor.

ドレッサーのトップ　　The dresser's top.

見晴らしの良い客室の窓は出窓になっている
The guest room's window is a bay window, commanding a fine view.

ブルーベルベットをテーマカラーにエレガンスな雰囲気を演出したスペシャリティ レストラン "Corintia"（65席）
The specialty restaurant "Corintia" (65 seats) features an elegant atmosphere with blue velvet as the theme color.

2階 "Corintia" の入口
The entrance to "Corintia" at the 2nd floor.

大きなエッチド グラスとテーブルセッティング
The large etched glass and table setting.

カクテル ラウンジ "Allegro"（65席）のカウンターをみる
The counter of the cocktail lounge "Allegro" (65 seats).

ルネッサンス スイートのリビングルーム

ベッドルーム

ダーク グリーンの落ち着いた店内　　　　The inside — composed mood with a dark green tone.

大理石を用いたリッチなバスルーム

(Photo captions)
From above:
● The living room of Renaissance suite room.
● The bedroom.
● The bathroom.

バンケット フロア最大規模の"Renaissance Ballroom"３つに分けられディナースタイルて400名収容てきる
"Renaissance Ballroom" — one of the largest banquet floors — partitioned into three segments, capable of accommodating 400 persons in a dinner style.

12階建　750室のホテルはロサンゼルス国際空港の近くに立地する
Having 750 rooms in 12 stories, this hotel stands close to Los Angeles International Airport.

STOUFFER
CONCOURSE HOTEL

5400 West Century Blvd. Los Angeles, CA 90045
Phone/213-216-5858

広いスペースのドライブ ウェイ　　The spacious driveway.

エントランスから広がるフロア　奥がレセプション

ホテルの裏側にある　アウト　ドア　プール

宴会ロビー

大宴会場(13,500sq.ft.)は3つに区分できる

ピアノの生演奏が流れる"ロビーコート"はエレガントなカクテル ラウンジ
"Lobby Court" is an elegant cocktail lounge where live piano music is on air.

2階宴会場フロアより開放的なロビーを見おろす
An open lobby viewed from the banquet hall at the 2nd floor.

"プレシデンタル スイート"のリビングルーム　　The living room of "Presidential Suite."

ホームバーの雰囲気のウェットバーが付いている

T.V.もあるラグジュアリータイプのバスルーム

(Photo captions)
Top / Provided with a wet bar having an atmosphere of a home bar.
Bottom / A luxury type bathroom equipped with a TV set.

マホガニー材を用いた重厚なベッドルーム　　A dignified bedroom using mahogany.

(Photo captions — page 68)
From above:
- The floor spreading from the entrance; at an inner part lies the reception.
- The outdoor pool behind the hotel.
- The banquet lobby.
- The large banquet hall (13,500 sq. ft.) can be partitioned into 3 segments.

ストゥファー コンコース ホテル

アメリカの大都市やリゾート地にファーストクラスのホ
テルを展開し現在30ヵ所となった「ストゥファーホテルズ
(本社オハイオ州ソロン)」がサンベルト地帯のキー シ
ティとしてアトランタ デンバー ロサンゼルスなどに最
近オープンした。
ロサンゼルス国際空港近くの同ホテルは 地上12階建750
室の規模であり エアポートホテルとしての機能に加え
最大1,500名を収容する大宴会場を備えるなど 大型コン
ベンションもできる多目的な都市型ホテルとして利用さ
れている。
メインダイニングであるレストランでは イタリア料理
を提供し インフォーマルなレストランでサンドイッチ
からローストビーフまで 幅広いメニューを用意するな
ど 当ホテルのフランス人の料理長やF・Bマネージャー
の鋭い情報分析に基づいたメニュー作りには 時代のニ
ーズにたえず目を向けている姿勢がうかがえる。
オープン/1987年10月18日
規模・客室数/地上12階建750室(内スイート47室)
料飲施設/3：Charisma Cafe(インフォーマルレストラン)
　　　　240席 Trattoria Grande(イタリア料理レスト
　　　　ラン)100席 Lobby Court(バーラウンジ)150
　　　　席
宴会・会議場/大宴会場(13,500sq.-ft.)
その他の施設/ヘルスクラブ 屋外プール

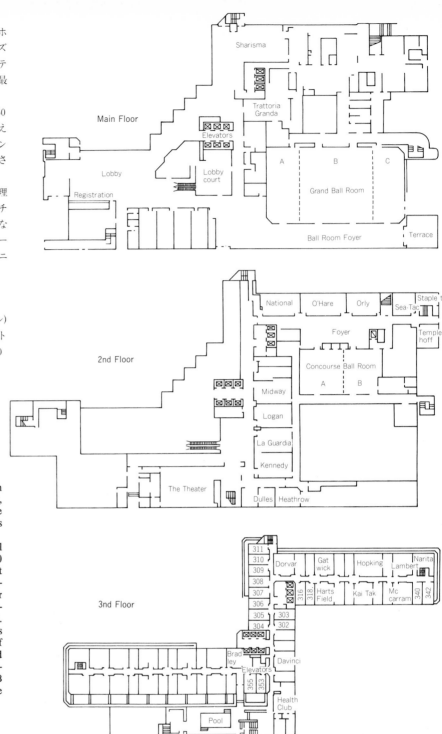

STOUFFER CONCOURSE HOTEL

Developing a chain of first class hotels in big American
cities and resorts, totalling 30 locations at present,
Stouffer Hotels (headquartered in Solon, Ohio) have
recently opened chain hotels in Atlanta, Denver, Los
Angeles, etc. which are key cities along the Sunbelt.
The hotel, located near Los Angeles International
Airport, is 12-storied above the ground, having 750
guest rooms. In addition to functions as an airport
hotel, it also has a banquet hall capable of accommodating 1,500 persons at maximum. Thus, "Stouffer
Concourse Hotel" is utilized as a multi-purpose city-
type hotel where a large-scale convention can be held.
At a restaurant which is the main dining, Italian dishes
are served. At an informal restaurant, a wide range of
dishes are on the menu, from sandwiches to roasted
beef. Thus, in the menu making based on keen information analysis made by a French chef and F·B
manager, an attitude always eyeing the needs of the
times can be observed.

5400 West Century Blvd., Los Angeles, CA 90045
Phone: 213-216-5858

Opened / October 18, 1986
Scale, number of guest rooms / 12 stories, 750 rooms
　(incl. 47 suite rooms)
Eating/drinking facilities / Charisma cafe
　(informal restaurant, 240 seats),
　Trattoria Grande (Italian restaurant, 100 seats),
　Lobby court (bar lounge, 150 seats)
Banquet hall, boardroom / Large banquet hall (capable
　of accommodating 1,500 persons),
　Boardrooms (33)
Other facilities / Health club, Outdoor pool

(Photo captions – page 71)
Top / "Club Lounge" provided at the highest floor. There, express check in/out service,
　breakfast and free hors d'œuvre service are offered.
Bottom / At the lounge which can be freely used by club floor guests, card telephone
　service is also available.

最上階フロアに設けられた"Club Lounge" エキスプレスチェックイン アウトサービス 朝食 オードブルの無料サービスを提供

クラブ フロア客が自由に利用できるラウンジはカード電話も利用できる

オールデイ ダイニングの"Charisma Cafe"（240席）より高い天井の店内をみる
The inside featuring a high ceiling, as viewed from all-day dining "Charisma Cafe" (240 seats).

ビュッフェ コーナーのある奥のダイニング エリア
The inner dining area where a buffet corner is provided.

朝 昼 夜の多目的ビュッフェが好評 空港という立地だけに利用者も多い
The multi-purpose buffet for morning, noon and night is very popular. Since this hotel stands near the airport, the buffet is used by many people.

店内中央に設けられたオープン キッチン

メイン ダイニングの"Trattoria Grande"（100席）はシーフードとパスタが中心
The main dining "Trattoria Grande" (100 seats) serves seafoods and pastas in the main.

オープン キッチン前のデザート ディスプレイ

入口付近よりテーブル席をみる　　　　The table seats viewed from the entrance area.

壁面には長い椅子を配し　料理はハーフサイズも注
文できる

(Photo captions)
Top / The open kitchen provided in the center.
Middle / The dessert display in front of the open kitchen.
Bottom / Long chairs are placed beside the wall. As for dishes, you can order a half size, too.

隣接した新しいショッピングセンター"Horton Plaza"と共に話題のホテル

ポストモダンとネオクラシックの外観をみる

(Photo captions)
Top / The topical hotel, side by side with the adjacent new shopping center "Horton Plaza."
Bottom / The postmodern plus neoclassic appearance.

OMNI ❁ SAN DIEGO HOTEL

1 Broadway Circle San Diego, CA 92101
Phone/619-239-2200

アトリウム空間をみる　左側の階段は2階の宴会　会議室へ通じる
A view of the atrium space. The left side staircase leads to the banquet hall and boardroom.

コンシアージデスクとフロント レセプション　The concierge desk and front reception.

オムニ サン ディエゴ ホテル

都市型ホテルとして全米にチェーンを展開する「Omni Hotels」は　現在までに25のホテルを運営しており　このサン ディエゴへの進出がチェーンでもっとも新しいホテルである。ダウンタウンにあって　新しいショッピングセンターの「Horton Plaza（120店）」に隣接　1989年の秋に完成予定の「サン ディエゴ コンベンション センター（250,000 sq.-ft.）」へ6ブロックという好立地のホテルでもある。デザインはポスト モダン　ネオクラシカルスタイル　サウスウエスト調などの要素をうまく取り入れている。ビストロ調のレストランやバイレベルのスイートルームを設けているのも特長だ。サン ディエゴという観光とビジネスの都市にこのところ　新しいホテルの進出が増えてきている。

オープン/1987年9月
規模・客室数/地上15階建452室（内スイート21室 バイレベルスイート4室）
料飲施設/4：Specialty Restaurant110席　Lobby Lounge36席　Cafe Bistro140席 Entertainment Lounge200席
宴会・会議場/大宴会場（9,000sq.-ft.）会議室11室
その他の施設/ヘルスクラブ（3,000sq.-ft.）屋外プール　サンデッキ 照明付屋外テニスコート（2面）

OMNI SAN DIEGO HOTEL

Omni Hotels has been developing its chain of city-type hotels across the U.S., and is currently operating 25 hotels. This hotel in San Diego is the latest in the chain. Open in the downtown, adjacent to "Horten Plaza" (120 shops), a new shopping center, and only 6 blocks distance from "San Diego Convention Center" (250,000 sq. ft.) to be completed in the fall of 1989, it thus is ideally located.

It has been designed by skillfully incorporating the postmodern, neoclassical and southwestern styles and elements. The hotel also features a bistroic restaurant and bi-level suite rooms. In San Diego – a city of tourism and business – an increasing number of new hotels are being opened.

1 Broadway Circle, San Diego, CA 92101
Phone: 619-239-2200

Opened / September 1987
Scale, number of guest rooms / 15 stories, 452 rooms
    (incl. 21 suite rooms and 4 bi-level suite rooms)
Eating/drinking facilities / Specialty restaurant
    (110 sests), Lobby lounge (36 seats),
    Cafe bist. (140 seats),
    Entertainment lounge (200 seats)
Banquet hall, boardroom / Large banquet hall
    (9,000 sq. ft.), Boardrooms (11)
Other facilities / Health club (3,000 sq. ft.),
    Outdoor pool, Sundeck, Outdoor tennis court with
    lighting (2 surfaces)

グラスドームが突き出したメインエントランス

カジュアル レストラン "Cafe Bistro"(140席)　　The casual restaurant "Cafe Bistro" (140 seats).

"Cafe Bistro"のオープンキッチン

ロビー ラウンジよりカウンターをみる

(Photo captions)
Top / The main entrance featuring a projected glass dome.
Middle / The open kitchen of "Cafe Bistro."
Bottom / The counter viewed from the lobby lounge.

バーラウンジ "Lobby Lounge"(36席)はライブ演奏も楽しめる
At the bar lounge "Lobby Lounge" (36 seats), you can also enjoy live music.

9,000sq.-ft.の大宴会場は3つに区分できる　1,200人のレセプションが可能
The huge (9,000 sq. ft.) banquet hall can be partitioned into 3 segments, where a reception of 1,200 persons is possible.

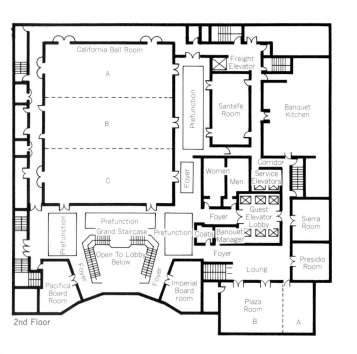

2nd Floor

3rd Floor

"Entertainment Lounge"（200席）のバー　カウンター　ＴＶモニターでスポーツやディスコのテープを流す
The bar counter of "Entertainment" (200 seats) where sports or disco tapes are displayed on TV monitors.

ＴＶモニターを設置したラウンジ
The lounge where TV monitors are installed.

中央がダンスフロアで周りがカウンターとテーブル席
The dance floor in the center, surrounded by the counter and table se

"Specialty Restaurant"（110席）はメイン ダイニング
"Specialty Restaurant" (110 seats) is the main dining.

中央がテーブル席で周りに個室が4つある
The table seats in the center, surrounded by 4 private rooms.

右上・右下・左上・左下／バイレベルのスイートルームをみる　マスターベッドルームは上の階にある
Left above, left bottom, right above, right bottom / A view of the bi-level suite room. The master bed is on the upper floor.

このエグゼクティブ ボードルームを含めて小会議室は11室ある

There are 11 small boardrooms, including this executive boardroom.

オフィスとホテルの複合として　最上部38〜48階までの11フロアーが客室
As an office-hotel composite operation, the highest 11 floors (from 38th to 48th) are occupied by guest rooms.

MANDARIN ORIENTAL
SAN FRANCISCO

222 Sansome Street San Francisco, CA 94104-2792
Phone／415-885-0999

1階"クリッパー ラウンジ"の近くにあるギフトショップ
The gift shop near "Clipper Lounge" at the 1st floor.

オリエンタル調のフロント レセプション エリア

The guest room in an Oriental style.

ティー カクテル 朝食 ランチなど多目的な営業をするロビー レヘルの"Clipper Lounge"（64席）
"Clipper Lounge" (64 seats) at the lobby level which is intended for multi-purpose services, such as tea, cocktail, breakfast and lunch.

メイン ダイニング"Silks"(74席)は朝食　ランチ　夕食を提供する
The main dining "Silks" (74 seats) serves breakfast, lunch and dinner.

"Silks"の花と果物　デザート類のディスプレイ
The display at "Silks" of flowers, fruits and desserts.

エントランスとドアマン　　The entrance and doorman.

ロビーレベル奥の"Mandarin Bar"(35席)
"Mandarin Bar"(35 seats) at an inner part of the lobby level.

調理長の Howa d Bulka 氏　　Mr. Howa d Bulka, chef.

ロビー レベルより2階レストランと宴会場へ通じる階段をみる
The staircase leading to the 2nd floor restaurant and banquet hall, viewed from the lobby level.

マンダリン オリエンタル サンフランシスコ

ホンコンを中心にアジアやカナダにも進出したホテルで グループ中10
番目のホテルとなった。サンフランシスコの商業と金融の中心街に建つ
48階建のオフィスビルの最上部11フロアを占める 大変見晴らしの良
い客室で構成している。全体で160室の客室は 各フロアに14室ずつ配
置され プライバシーや静かさを保てるようにも配慮されている。大理
石をふんだんに使用したバスルームも広く ここからも眺望を楽しめる
ようになっている。料飲施設やバンケット施設にも 素晴らしいテーブ
ルセッティングとサービスがなされており 世界のトップクラスのホテ
ルとして 高く評価されている。その独特のコンセプトを持ち込んでい
る。

デベロッパー/Norland Properties
経営/Mandarin Oriental Hotel Group, Hong Kong
設計/建築・Skidmore, Owings & Merrill
　　　内装・Don Ashton
オープン/1987年5月
規模・客室数/地上48階建(38〜48階の11フロアーをホテルとして使用)
　　　160室
料飲施設/3：Silks Dining Room(レストラン)74席　Clipper Lounge(ラ
　　　ウンジ)64席　Mandarin Bar(バー)35席
宴会・会議場/宴会場：Embassy Room(1,400sq.-ft.)
　　　　　　Library(1,100sq.-ft.)　Boardroom(1,000sq.-ft.)
その他の施設/ヘルスクラブ(5,000sq.-ft.)

MANDARIN ORIENTAL, SAN FRANCISCO

This hotel chain is mainly operating in Hong Kong, and has also
advanced into Asia, Canada, etc. This hotel in San Francisco is 10th
largest in the group. It occupies 11 floors at the highest part of
a 48-storied office building standing at the central street of commerce
and finance in San Francisco. Commanding a very fine view, it has
a total of 160 guest rooms, with 14 rooms arranged at each floor and
considerations given to maintain privacy and quietness. A bathroom,
using abundant marble, is spacious, from which you can also enjoy
a fine view. Eating/drinking and banqueting facilities also come with
wonderful table setting and services. Thus, this hotel is highly reputed
as one of the top-class hotels in the world. This chain's unique concept is also incorporated in this hotel.

222 Sansome Street, San Francisco, CA 94104-2792
Phone: 415-885-0999

Developer / Norland Properties
Owner / Mandarin Oriental Hotel Group, Hong Kong
Design / Architecture: Skidmore, Owings & Merrill
　　　Interior: Don Ashton
Opened / May 1987
Scale, number of guest rooms / 48 stories (11 floors from 38th to 48th
　　　are used as a hotel), 160 rooms
Eating/drinking facilities / Silks dining room (restaurant, 74 seats),
　　　Clipper lounge (lounge, 64 seats), Mandarin bar (bar, 35 seats)
Banquet hall, boardroom / Banquet halls: Embassy room
　　　(1,400sq. ft.), Library (1,100 sq. ft.); Boardroom (1,000 sq. ft.)
Other facilities / Health club (5,000 sq. ft.)

宴会場への通路 パブリック フォーンが設置してある

The passage leading to the banquet hall. Public phones are installed.

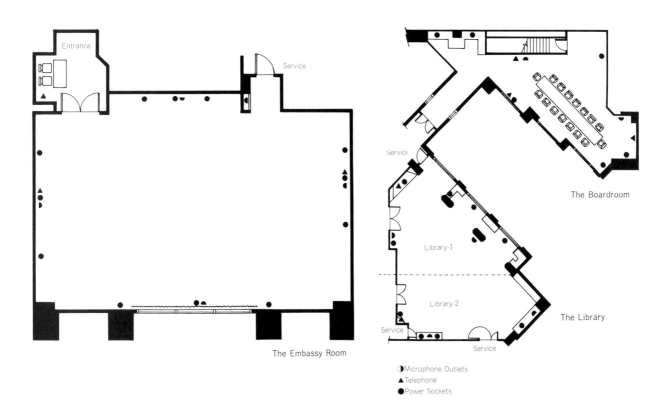

The Embassy Room

The Boardroom

The Library

Library-1

Library-2

Entrance

Service

Service

Service

Service

Service

◖ Microphone Outlets
▲ Telephone
● Power Sockets

大宴会場"Embassy Room"（1,400sq.·ft.）

The large banquet hall "Embassy Room" (1,400 sq. ft.).

書斎風にした宴会場"Library"（1,100sq.·ft.）
The banquet hall "Library" (1,100 sq. ft.), in a study style.

会議室"Board Room"（1,000sq.·ft.）
The boardroom "Board Room" (1,000 sq. ft.).

スイートルーム　　　The suite room.

48階のベッドルームと夜景　　The bedroom and night scene of the 48th floor.

スイートのマスター ベッドルーム
The suite master bed.

オリエンタル調の客室　　The front reception area in an Oriental style.

上・下/ゴージャスなバスルームは見晴らしやアメニティも素晴しい
(Photo captions)
Top, bottom / The gorgeous bathroom features a wonderful view and amenities.

Moscone Convention Center 近くに立地し　36階建　675室のホテルの外観（中央）
The appearance of the 36-storied hotel, having 675 rooms (in the center), located near Moscone Convention Center.

HOTEL
MERIDIEN
SAN FRANCISCO

50 Third Street San Francisco, CA 94103
Phone/415-974-6400

エントランスホール　　　　　　　The entrance hall.

最上階の3フロアはVIP用の"Club Privilege"
The three highest floors are occupied by "Club Privilege" for VIP's.

ロビーより左にフロント レセプション　右にメイン エントランスをみる
The front reception in the left side of the lobby.　In the right side lies the main entrance hall.

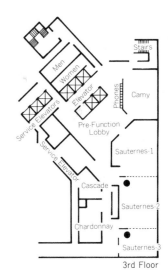

3rd Floor

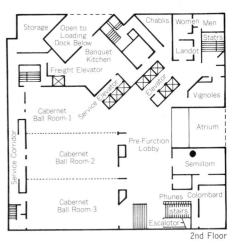

レセプション廻り

The reception area.

2nd Floor

"Justin" カジュアル レストランとして軽食とシーフード料理が楽しめる
"Justin" — a casual restaurant where you can enjoy tasting light meals and seafood dishes.

ステージ状にレイアウトされた店内　　　The inside laid out like a stage.

バー ラウンジ　　　The bar lounge.

"Pierre" 高級フランス料理を提供するこの店はあのアラン シャペルが指導している
"Pierre" – Serving high-grade French dishes, this restaurant is operated at the instructions of Alain Chapel, a well-known chef.

"Pierre"に併設されたバー ラウンジ
The bar lounge attached to "Pierre."

ゆったりとした客席　落ち着いた店内
The comfortable guest seats in a composed atmosphere.

大宴会場（10,000sq.-ft.）と小宴会場及び会議室が15室ある
There are a large (10,000 sq. ft.) banquet hall, a small banquet hall and 15 boardrooms.

ホテル メリディアン サンフランシスコ

「ホテル メリディアン チェーン」は1972年エールフランスのホテル部門より独立し 現在では世界40数都市に50以上のホテルを有するインターナショナル ホテル チェーンとして発展を続けている。同チェーンはまたアメリカへの進出を積極的に展開しており このサンフランシスコのホテルは モントリオール ヒューストン ニューヨークやボストンに次いで5番目 全体では43番目のものとなった。市の中心に立地し「モスコーン コンベンションセンター」の近くにある36階建675室を有する同ホテルはビジネスマンから政治家と幅広い層に利用されている。フレンチスタイルの洗練されたサービスとすぐれた諸施設が好評である。特にレストラン「ピエール（Pierre）」は有名なシェフ アラン シャペルの采配の下で アメリカに本格的なフランス料理を導入している。

オープン/1983年10月

規模・客室数/地上36階建675室

料飲施設/レストラン2 バー2

宴会・会議場/大会議室（10,000sq.-ft.950人収容）バンケット＆ミーティングルーム15室

総投資額/9,000万ドル

HOTEL MERIDIEN SAN FRANCISCO

In 1972 the Hotel Meridian chain became independent from the hotel division of Air France. Since then, it has developed into an international hotel chain, with more than 50 hotels in 40 or more cities in the world at present.

The chain is also developing actively its operations in the U.S., and this hotel in San Francisco is the 5th in the U.S., following those in Montreal, Houston, New York and Boston, and the 43rd of the whole chain.

Located in the center of the city, close to "Moscone Convention Center," this 36-storied hotel has 675 rooms, while being patronized by many guests, from businessmen to politicians. Its refined French style services and excellent facilities are highly reputed. The restaurant "Pierre," among others, is introducing traditional French dishes into the U.S., under the supervision of a well-known chef, Alain Chapel.

50, Third Street, San Francisco, CA 94103
Phone: 415-974-6400

Opened / October 1983
Scale, number of guest rooms / 36 stories, 675 rooms
Eating/drinking facilities / Restaurants (2), bars (2)
Banquet hall, boardroom / Large conference room (10,000 sq. ft., capable of accommodating 950 persons), Banquet & meeting rooms (15)
Total investment / $90 million

見晴らしの良い大きな窓

プレジデンシャル スイートのリビングルーム　The living room of a presidential suite room.

広いスペースのバスルーム

素晴らしいアメニティも揃っている

ゴージャスな家具　調度品が備わっている　Equipped with gorgeous furniture and utensils.

(Photo captions)
Top / The large window commanding a fine view.
Middle / The spacious bathroom.
Bottom / Wonderful amenities are also available.

もう1つのプレジデンシャル スイートの広いリビングルーム
The wide living room of another presidential suite room.

ウェットバーよりスイートをみる
The suite room viewed from the wet bar.

御影石　ライム ストーン　光沢のあるブリックなどを使用した９階建ホテルの外観
The appearance of the hotel using granite, limestone, glossy bricks, etc.

THE WESTIN HOTEL
Washington, D.C.

2401 M Street N.W. Washington D.C. 20037
Phone / 202-429-2400

コートヤードに面したレストラン"The Colonnade"
"The Colonnade" – a restaurant facing the coutyard.

エレガントな雰囲気のエントランスホール

中2階よりロビーラウンジをみる

イタリア式の泉を設けたガーデンコート

(Photo captions)
Top / The entrance hall having an elegant atmosphere.
Middle / The lobby lounge viewed from the mezzanine.
Bottom / The garden court featuring an Italian fountain.

ガーデンコートに面したラウンジ　　　The lounge facing the garden court.

オープンバーの周りにラウンジが展開する　Lounges are arranged around the open bar.

"The Bistro"のバーコーナー　　　"The Bistro's" bar corner.

"The Colonnade"の開放的なダイニング エリア
The open dining area of "The Colonnade."

"The Colonnade"の外観　　**The appearance of "The Colonnade."**

入口よりブース席をみる　**The booth seats viewed from the entrance.**

フランスのビストロを表現したダイニング エリア
The dining area expressing a bistro in France.

バーとダイニングが一緒になってカジュアルな雰囲気
A casual atmosphere in which the bar and dining room are one.

最大500名の大宴会場(5,460sq.-ft.)

The large banquet hall (5,400 sq. ft.) accommodating 500 persons at maximum.

ザ ウェスティン ホテル ワシントン D. C.

アメリカの首都コロンビア特別区ワシントンD.C.に開業した同ホテルは ワシントンの伝統的な建築様式をとり入れ 御影石や石灰石 ガラスの ブリックなどを使用した外観となっている。中庭を設けてその中央に三 層のイタリア式噴水を置くなど ユーロピアンタイプのリゾート性あふ れる雰囲気も持ち込んでいる。

416室の客室のうち146室はこの中庭に面しており パステル調の色を生 かした エレガントなデコレイトになっている。電話も部屋に2ヵ所と バスルームに備えている。

コンベンションの多い所として それらに対応できる諸設備 大宴会場 シアター形式のエグゼクティブ フォーラム さらにテレビによる会議が できるシステムまで導入している。

オープン/1983年12月16日

規模・客室数/地上9階建416室(内スイート34室 特別室3室)

料飲施設/ファインダイニング1 ビストロ1 ロビーラウンジ1

宴会・会議場/宴会場14室(大宴会場5,460sq.-ft.Executive Forum シア ター185席)

その他の施設/Fitness Center(16,000sq.-ft. 屋内プール スクアッシュ
コート ウエイトルーム エアロビクス サウナ シャワー
ジ マッサージルーム など含む)

THE WESTIN HOTEL, Washington D.C.

This hotel, opened in Washington D.C., the capital of the U.S., features a traditional architectural style local to Washington, making use of granite, limestone and glass bricks. It is provided with a courtyard with an Italian three-layer fountain placed at its center, to offer to the guests the feeling of a European atmosphere.

Of the 416 guest rooms, 146 face the courtyard. Each room is decorated elegantly with pastel colors, and is equipped with two phones inside the room and one in the bathroom.

A variety of facilities, a large banquet hall, theater style executive forum as well as a system for TV conference are available for a great number of conventions that are held frequently in this area.

2401, M Street, N.W. Washington, D.C. 20037
Phone: 202-429-2400

Opened / December 16, 1985

Scale, number of guest rooms / 9 stories, 416 rooms (incl. 34 suite rooms, and 3 special rooms)

Eating/drinking facilities / Fine dining rooms, bistro, lobby lounge

Banquet hall, boardroom / Banquet halls (14) (incl. large banquet hall (5,460 sq. ft.), Executive forum (theater, 185 seats))

Other facilities / Fitness center (16,000 sq. ft., incl. an indoor pool, squash court, waiting room, aerobics room, sauna room, shower room, massage room, etc.)

Ball Room Floor

Westin Ball Room
South   North

Meeting Room

A B C

Executive Forum

Prefunction

D

E

Westin Fitness Center

G F

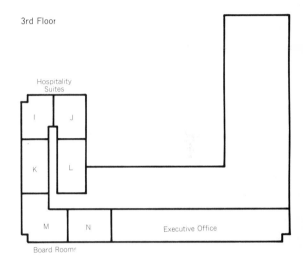

3rd Floor

Hospitality Suites

I J

K L

M N

Executive Office

Board Rooms

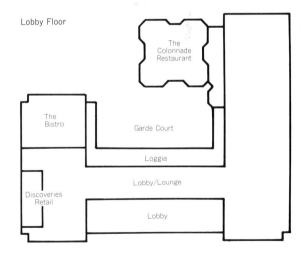

Lobby Floor

The Colonnade Restaurant

The Bistro

Garde Court

Loggia

Lobby/Lounge

Discoveries Retail

Lobby

シアター式の"Executive Forum"（185名）
The theater-style "Executive Forum" (accommodating 185 persons).

宴会場ロビーはレセプション エリアとして利用
The banquet hall's lobby is used as a reception area.

プレジデンシャル スイートのリビングルーム　　　　　The living room of a presidential suite room.

マスター ヘッドルーム　　　The master bedroom.

キングサイズのマスター ヘッドルーム　The master bedroom of a king size.

スイートのリビングルーム

The bedroom of a suite room.

左下/右下/"The Westin Fitness Center" スカッシュ コート スイミングプール サウナ エクササイズ ルームなどがある
Left bottom, right bottom / "The Westin Fitness Center" – a squash court, swimming pool, sauna room, exercise room, etc. are available.

ロビーよりフロント レセプションをみる   The front reception viewed from the lobby.

周りの環境に合せ4階建と低層
The building is low (4 stories) harmonizing with the surrounding environment.

SAN FRANCISCO
Marriott.
FISHERMAN'S WHARF

1250 Columbus Avenue San Francisco, CA 94133
Phone/415-775-7555

102

ロビーバーのカウンターをみる
The counter viewed from the lobby bar.

ロビーよりロビー ラウンジへと導くエレガントな雰囲気
An elegant atmosphere leading from the lobby to the lobby lounge.

右下・右下／"Wellington's Restaurant"はメスキート（Mesquite）ブロイルのステーキやシーフードを提供する
Left bottom, right bottom / "Wellington's Restaurant" serves mesquite-broiled steak and seafoods.

ドライブウェイから入口をみる
The entrance viewed from the driveway.

マリオット フィッシャーマンズ ワーフ S.F.
サンフランシスコの観光スポットとして知られるフィッシャーマンズ ワーフ地区に進出した同ホテルは レジデンシャル ホテルとして客室の半分以上をキングサイズレベルのデラックスさで構成している。外観は周囲の環境に合わせ4階建と低層棟になっており 内部は豪華な客室 エレガントな雰囲気のロビーなどと共に格調のある料飲施設を配している。特に一段と広いスペースをとったエンターテイメント ラウンジはスカイライトを導入したセンスの良いバーである。
徒歩圏内の距離に「ギラデリー スクエア」「ザ キャナリィ」などのスペシャリティ ショップやレストランの集まる観光名所もあり ビジネスや観光の目的で利用されている。
オープン/1984年8月3日
規模・客席数/地上4階建256室（内スイート12室 キングルーム97室）
料飲施設/レストラン1 バーラウンジ2

MARRIOTT FISHERMAN'S WHARF, S.F.

This hotel, opened at Fisherman's Wharf well known as a tourist spot in San Francisco, is a residential hotel and more than 50% of its guest rooms are deluxe and king-sized. To harmonize with the surrounding environment, the building itself is low (only 4 stories), and inside the building are arranged deluxe guest rooms, elegant lobbies, and refined eating/drinking facilities. A spacious entertainment lounge, among others, is a tasteful bar featuring a skylight.
Within walking distance can be found a place of interests where specialty shops and restaurants are arranged, such as "Giladilly Square" and "The Canary." This hotel is suitable for business and sightseeing purposes.

1250, Columbus Avenue, San Francisco, CA 94133
Phone: 415-775-7555

Opened / August 3, 1984
Scale, number of guest rooms / 4 stories, 256 rooms (incl. 12 suite rooms, 97 king rooms)
Eating/drinking facilities / Restaurant (1), Bar lounges (2)

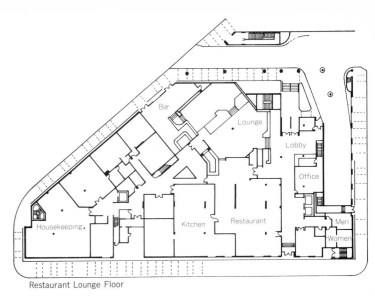

Restaurant Lounge Floor

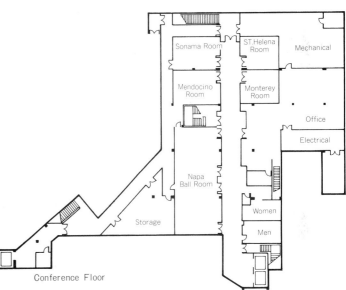

Conference Floor

スカイライトを導入したバー "Illusions" は同ホテル内で最大のスペースをもっている
The bar "Illusions" featuring a skylight has the largest space within the hotel.

広いスペースのバーとハッピーアワーのためのオードブル類がディスプレイされているバーラウンジ "Illusions"

変化のある客席とリッチなテーブルトップのバーラウンジ
The varied guest seats and bar lounge featuring a rich tabletop.

97室あるキングサイズの客室　　　　　　　　　　　　　One of 97 king-size guest rooms.

The spacious bar lounge and hors d'œuvre for happy hour at "Illusions."

上・左下／スペシャル キングルームのシックなコーディネーション

Top, left bottom / A chic coordination of special king rooms.

全室バルコニーを設けた16階建285室を有するソフト ベージュの外観
The soft beige appearance of the 16-storied hotel having 285 rooms all of which have a balcony.

FourSeasonsHotel
AT BEVERLY HILLS

300 S. Doheny Drive Los Angeles, CA 90048
Phone/213-273-2222

エントランスとドライブ ウエイ
The entrance and driveway.

エントランスの正面をみる　A front view of the entrance.

ベル キャプテン カウンター　The bell captain counter.

エレガントなフロント廻り　The elegant front area.

フロント レセプション廻り　ルイ16世紀の頃より現代までの家具　調度類を配している

The front reception area where furniture and utensils from the days of Louis XVI to date are arranged.

フォーマル ダイニング ルーム "Gardens"

The formal dining room "Gardens."

左が"Gardens" 右が"The Cafe"（インフォーマル）
"Gardens" at left and "The Cafe" (informal) at right.

シルバー グレーとバター イエローの"Gardens"
"Gardens" with silver grey and butter yellow.

"The Bar" 2つの大きな窓を配しカウンターとテーブルが展開する

"The Bar" featuring two large windows and counter/table arrangement.

"Windows" と呼ぶソフトローズを配したラウンジ
The lounge called "Windows" featuring soft rose coloring.

18世紀のフランス式窓を配したバーカウンター
The bar counter where the 18th centurial French window is arranged.

フォー シーズンズ ホテル ロサンゼルス

カナダに本社を置く「フォー シーズンズ ホテルズ」は 現在までにカナダ アメリカ イギリスに22のホテルを展開している。格調の高さとエレガンス サービスなどに最も力を入れているホテルとしても好評である。
ロサンゼルスのビバリーヒルズ地区に13年ぶりに新しく開業したホテルとして注目されている。インテリア デザインを担当したLouis Cataffo氏はパブリックエリアは全てエレガントなアーチの窓を透すことで外の眺めを引き立て フランスの伝統的な家具に合わせパラディアン シンメトリィを持ち込んだり グレイや黒 ゴールデンハニーといった色調でカリフォルニアでは稀なエレガンスを表現したという。そしてフランスのシャトーに見られるアンティークの彫刻や家具 ファイアープレイスなどもヨーロッパから求めている。これらの芸術品と照明などにより伝統的なヨーロッパの雰囲気を表現するホテルとなっている。
設計/建築・Gin Wong Assosiates, L.A.
　　　内装・Intradesign, L.A.
オープン/1987年4月16日
規模・客室数/地上16階建285室(内スイート106室)
料飲施設/4：Gardens(レストラン) Windows(レストラン＆バー)
　　　　Cafe(レストラン) プールサイドレストラン など
宴会場・会議室/宴会場7 (大宴会場4,200sq.-ft.)
その他の施設/屋外プール フィットネスセンター

テーマカラーのソフトグリーンを用いたエレベーターホール
The elevator hall using the theme color – soft green.

FOUR SEASONS HOTEL, Los Angeles

"Four Seasons Hotel," with headquarters in Canada, is currently developing a chain of 22 hotels in Canada, the U.S. and U.K. These hotels are highly reputed for their high-class, elegance and excellent services.
This hotel is drawing attention, as it has opened after a long interval (13 years) in Beverly Hills, Los Angeles. Mr. Louis Cataffo, who designed the interior, said that the outside view has been made attractive by arranging the entire public square to be seen through elegant arch windows, and a Palladian symmetry has been incorporated to harmonize with the traditional French furniture, using grey, black, golden honey, etc., and expressing thus an elegance rare in California. Antique sculpture, furniture, fireplace, etc., which are available in châteaux in France, have also been brought from Europe. Thanks to these art works, lighting, etc., this hotel expresses a traditional European atmosphere.

300, S. Doheny Drive, Los Angeles, CA 90048
Phone: 213-273-2222

Design / Architecture: Gin Wong Associates (L.A.)
　　Interior: Intradesign (L.A.)
Opened / April 16, 1987
Scale, number of guest rooms / 16 stories, 285 rooms (incl. 106 suite rooms)
Eating/drinking facilities / Gardens (restaurant), Windows (restaurant & bar), Cafe (restaurant), Poolside restaurant, etc.
Banquet hall, boardroom / Banquet halls (7) (incl. large banquet hall (4,200 sq. ft.))
Other facilities / Outdoor pool, Fitness center

大きなシャンデリアのあるミーティングルーム
The meeting room having large chandeliers.

左頁下・115頁／プレジデンシャル スイートルーム　ヨーロッパの伝統にカリフォルニアのコンテンポラリーが加わったデザイン
Left page bottom, page 115 / A presidential suite room whose design is a combination of traditional European and contemporary Californian elements.

プールに併設した軽食サービスのテラス レストラン

The terrace restaurant beside the pool, serving light meals.

プールサイドのアウト ドアのエクササイズ施設

The outdoor exercise facilities on the poolside.

円形シェードを配した屋外プール

The outdoor pool featuring circular shades.

21階建 397室　窓を大きくとった外観

The appearance of the 21-storied hotel having 397 rooms, featuring large windows.

H O T E L
MERIDIEN
VANCOUVER

845 Burrard at Robson Vancouver, B.C.V6Z ZK6 Canada
Phone/604-682-5511

エレベーターホール　　　The elevator hall.

1階ロビー エリア ヨーロッパの伝統的なレジデンシャル スタイルのホテルとして好評
The 1st floor lobby area. This hotel is highly reputed as a traditional European residential-style hotel.

ロビーにあるクロークと右は客室へのエレベーターホール

照明も落ち着いた感じのフロント廻り

ロビーのコンシアージ デスクと2階の宴会 会議室への階段

(Photo captions)
Top / The cloakroom at the lobby. At right is the elevator hall leading to guest rooms.
Left bottom / The front area whose lighting has a composed atmosphere.
Right bottom / The concierge desk at the lobby and the staircase leading to the 2nd floor where there are banquet halls and boardrooms.

左上・右上/ヘルスクラブとインドアプール
Right top, left top / The health club and indoor pool.

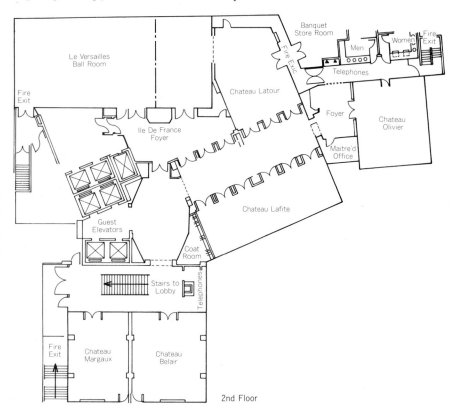
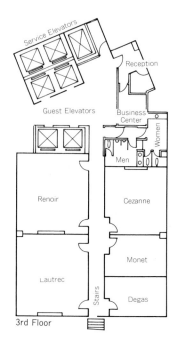

2nd Floor

3rd Floor

ホテル メリディアン バンクーバー

「メリディアン（フランス語で"子午線"の意）ホテルズ」は フランス本国を中心にヨーロッパ 北米 中東 アフリカ アジア 南米など 54軒1万9,100室のデラックス ホテルを展開している。"フレンチ タッチ"を売り物に洗練された料理とサービスで定評がある。

チェーン中51番目にあたるこのホテルは カナダのブリティッシュ コロンビア州バンクーバーに1986年1月にオープン。その5ヵ月後に開催された国際交通博覧会に向けて バンクーバーではホテルラッシュとなった。

インテリア デザインは同ホテルの「ニューポート ビーチ」やロサンゼルスの「Bel Airホテル」などのLouis Cataffo氏によるもの。ヨーロッパの伝統的なレジデンシャル スタイルのホテルとして 好評である。本格的なフランス料理レストランや ビジネス客のための会議室 最新の通信と情報設備を備えたビジネスセンターなども設けられている。

オープン/1986年1月2日

規模・客室数/地上21階建397室（内スイート46室 エグゼクティブルーム17室）

料飲施設/レストラン2 バー＆ラウンジ2

宴会・会議場/宴会場12室（エグゼクティブ コンファレンスルーム5室を含む）

その他の施設/ヘルスクラブビューティセンター ビジネス＆コミュニケーションセンター など

HOTEL MERIDIEN VANCOUVER

The Meridien Hotels ("Méridien" means the meridian in French) have developed as a chain mainly in France, and are operating currently in Europe, North America, the Middle East, Africa, Asia, Latin America, etc., with 54 hotels that include 19,100 deluxe rooms. With their "French touch" as a sale-point, these hotels are reputed for refined dishes and services.

The 51st of the chain, this hotel opened in January 1986 in Vancouver, State of British Columbia, Canada. In those days, with the International Traffic Exposition to be held 5 months later, a hotel construction boom took place in Vancouver.

The interior design has been undertaken by Mr. Louis Cataffo, who also took care of the interior design of "New Port Beach" of the same chain, "Bel Air Hotel" in Los Angeles, etc. As a hotel following the traditional European residential style, this hotel is highly reputed. It is provided with a traditional French restaurant, conference rooms for businessmen, a business center provided with the latest communication and information facilities, etc.

845, Burrard at Robson, Vancouver, B.C. V6Z ZK6 Canada
Phone: 604-682-5511

Opened / January 2, 1986
Scale, number of guest rooms / 21 stories, 397 rooms (incl. 46 suite rooms and 17 executive rooms)
Eating/drinking facilities / Restaurants (2), Bar & lounges (2)
Banquet hall, boardroom / Banquet halls (12) (incl. 5 executive conference rooms)
Other facilities / Health club, beauty center, business & communication center, etc.)

上・左上・右上/"Le Versailles Ballroom"（2分割可能）右下をはじめエグゼクティブ コンファレンス ルーム室を含む会議室　宴会場が12ヶ所ある

Top, right top, left top / "Le Versailles Ballroom" (can be divided into two). There are 12 boardrooms and banquet halls, including executive conference rooms (incl. the one shown at the right bottom).

"Restaurant Gerald"の個室（12名）　　A private room (12 persons) of "Restaurant Gerald."

"Restaurant Gerald"のメインダイニングルーム

"Bar Gerald"のカウンター　　"Bar Gerald's" counter.

"Bar Gerald"（50席）のラウンジ

The main dining room of "Restaurant Gerald."

豪華なシャンデリアのテーブル席

(Photo captions)
Left / "Bar Gerald's" lounge.
Right / The table seats under
gorgeous chandeliers.

レストランとバーの入口廻り
The entrance area of the restaurant and bar.

ブラッセリータイプのレストラン"Cafe Fleuri"（160席）
The brasserie type restaurant "Cafe Fleuri" (160 seats).

"La Promenade"（30席）はランチ サービスとティーやカクテルを提供する
"La Promenade" (130 seats) serves lunch, tea or cocktail.

上・下・左下／プレジデンシャル スイート ルーム　ヨーロッパの伝統家具やファイヤープレスを備えている

(Photo captions)
Top, bottom, left bottom / Presidential suite rooms, equipped with traditional
    European furniture, fireplace, etc.

オフィスとショッピングセンター　ホテルなどコンプレックスビルのエントランスが並んだファサード
The facade along which there are entrances of the complex building, including offices, shopping center and hotel.

⌀mfac Hotel

30 South 7th Street Minneapolis, Minnesota 55402
Phone/612-349-4000

エントランスとドアマン　　　　The entrance and doorman.

126

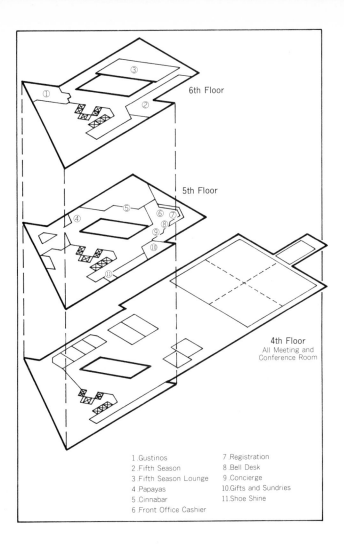

6th Floor

5th Floor

4th Floor
All Meeting and
Conference Room

1.Gustinos
2.Fifth Season
3.Fifth Season Lounge
4.Papayas
5.Cinnabar
6.Front Office Cashier
7.Registration
8.Bell Desk
9.Concierge
10.Gifts and Sundries
11.Shoe Shine

アムファック ホテル

「アムファック ホテルズ」はサンフランシスコを中心に全米に都市型と
リゾート型のホテルを約20ヵ所に展開している。いずれもユニークなア
イデアに基づいた施設構成が特徴で 注目されているチェーンホテルの
一つである。
ミネソタ州ミネアポリス市に完成した「ミネアポリス シティセンター オ
フィス＆リテイル コンプレックス」の一角を占めるこのホテルは 都市
再開発計画の一部であり 文字通りオフィスとショッピングセンター ホ
テルなどで構成する市の新しい名所となった。セミ リフレクティブ グ
ラスカーテンウォールを壁面に配した三角形の外観は32階建で602室を
有し ダイナミックなアトリウムロビーの周辺にレストランやバーラウ
ンジ 宴会場などのスペースを構成している。高級感 開放感を前面に
うち出している現代感覚溢れる都市型ホテルである。
設計(内装)/Cardennes/Darrall Associates of Santa Monica,CA
オープン/1983年11月1日
規模・客室数/地上32階建606室(内 バイ レベルエグゼクティブスイー
 ト23室)
料飲施設/レストラン3 バー＆ラウンジ2
宴会・会議/大宴会場(1,500人収容4F) 会議室8室
投資額/8,000万ドル

AMFAC HOTEL

The "AMFAC Hotels" chain, mainly developed in San Francisco,
is operating both urban-type and resort-type hotels at about 20
locations across the U.S. These hotels are characterized by their
common features, such as configuration of facilities based on unique
ideas.
Occupying part of the "Minneapolis City Eenter Office & Retail
Complex" which has been completed in Minneapolis City, State of
Minneapolis, this hotel is incorporated in the urban redevelopment
plan, and became a new place of interests in the city, that includes
offices, shopping center, hotel facilities, etc. This hotel, with its
triangular shape and semi-reflective glass curtain walls, has 32 stories,
equipped with 602 rooms and a space for restaurants, bar lounges,
banquet halls, etc. that surround the dynamic atrium lobby. This
urban-type hotel is full of modern feeling, featuring a high-class, open
atmosphere.

30, South 7th Street, Minneapolis, Minnesota, 55402
Phone: 612-349-4000

Design (interior) / Cardennes / Darrall Associates of Santa Monica, CA
Opened / November 1, 1983
Scale, number of guest rooms / 32 stories above, 606 rooms
 (incl. 23 bi-level executive suite rooms)
Eating/drinking facilities / Restaurants (3), Bar & lounges (2)
Banquet hall, boardroom / Large banquet hall (at the 4th floor,
 capable of accommodating 1,500 persons), Boardrooms (8)
Investment / $80 million

1階のエレベーターホール　　The elevator hall at the 1st floor.

ダイナミックなアトリウム ロビーよりパブリック スペースをみる　　　　The public space viewed from the dynamic atrium lobby.

落ち着いた広がりをみせる5階フロント ロビー

機能的にレイアウトしたフロント レセプション

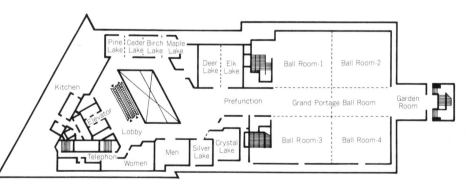

4th Floor

(Photo captions)
Top / The 5th floor front lobby having a composed expanse.
Bottom / The front reception featuring functional layout.

カジュアルなレストラン"Papaya's"の全景（5階）
The entire scene of the casual restaurant "Papaya's" (15th floor).

上/現代感覚を各所にとり入れたパブリックスペース
　宴会場やレストランを結ぶエスカレーターと奥に
　カジュアル レストラン"Papaya's"がみえる
左/"Papaya's"入口のディスプレイ

(Photo captions)
Top / The public space incorporating a modern sense. The escalator connecting banquet halls and restaurants is visible, together with the casual restaurant "Papaya's" at an inner part.
Left / The display at "Papaya's" entrance.

"Papaya's"のテーブル席　　　　　The table seats at "Papaya's."

外よりレストラン"The Fifth Season"をみる　　"The Fifth Season" viewed from the outside.

アメリカン キュイジーヌをメインにしたレストラン"The Fifth"
The restaurant "The Fifth" serving American cuisine in the main.

大宴会場のテーブルセッティッグ

入口より"Gustion's"の店内をみる　　"Gustion's" viewed from the entrance.

シックな雰囲気の"The Fifth Season Lounge"
"The Fifth Season Lounge" having a chic atmosphere.

北イタリア料理を提供するオペラ レストラン"Gustion's"はウエイターやウエイト
レスが歌うショータイムがある

(Photo captions)
Middle above / The table setting at the large banquet hall.
Middle bottom / The opera restaurant "Gustion's" serving North Italian
　　dishes. It has a show time when waiters and waitresses sing.

"バイレベル エグゼクティブ スイート"は最上階に23室ある　上階にベッドルーム　下階にバーコーナーを備えたパーラーで構成している

There are 23 "bi-level executive suite" rooms at the highest floor. Each room consists of a bedroom at the upper level, and a parlor with a bar corner at the lower level.

エントランスとドアマン　　　　　　　　　　The entrance and doorman.

メインストリード"ピーチトゥリー ストリード"に面した25階建の外観
The appearance of the 25-storied hotel facing the main street "Peachtree Street."

フロント レセプション　右奥がホテルのエントランス　　　　　　The front reception. At an inner part of the right is visible the hotel's entrance.

THE RITZ-CARLTON
ATLANTA

181 Peachtree Street, NE Atlanta, GA 30303　Phone/404-659-0400

クラブの雰囲気をもつ"The Restaurant"（90席）

"The Restaurant" (90 seats) having a club-like mood.

ライオンをデザインした大きな丸窓のあるエントランスホール
The entrance hall featuring a large spherical window which designs a lion.

パーソナル コンピューターを備えた コンシアージ デスク
The concierge desk equipped with a personal computer.

"Lobby Lounge"(31席)は朝食　ティーサービス　カクテルなどを提供する

"Lobby lounge" (31 seats) offers breakfast, tea service, cocktail, etc.

ザ リッツカールトン アトランタ

ジョージア州アトランタのピーチトゥリー ストリートに面し　大理石を使
用し　優雅なたたずまいを見せる地上25階建454室を有するホテルであ
る。超一流のサービスと格調を誇る同チェーンを象徴するごとく　料飲
施設から客室　宴会場施設まで充実した構成を見せている。毎週2,500本
の花々をホテル内のパブリックエリアや客室などに飾り　デザインの一
部として強調したり　食品やローストカート ダック プレスといったも
のに銀製品を多用しており　そのために4人の専任スタッフを置き24
時間磨き続けている。その他　利用客のニーズに対応したコンシアージ
(Concierge)サービスを徹底するなど　ビジネス個人客を中心にしたエグ
ゼクティブ層の開拓に力を入れている。
設計(内装)/Frank Nicholson Inc.Concord Massachusetts
オープン/1984年4月
規模・客室数/地上25階建454室(内スイート24室)
料飲施設/3：The Restaurant. The Cafe. Lobby Lounge.
宴会・会議場/会議室15室(7,412sq.-ft.ボードルーム2室 ホスピタリテ
　　ィ　スイート2室　コンファレンス　スイート3室を含む)

THE RITZ-CARLTON ATLANTA

Facing the Peachtree Street in the center of Atlanta, Georgia, and
using marble, this elegant hotel has 25 stories above the ground, with
454 guest rooms. To express the chain's claim of first-class services
and rank, all facilities, including those for eating/drinking purposes,
guest rooms and banquet halls, are neatly arranged.
To stress the presence of flowers as part of the overall design, 2,500
flowers are used every week to decorate public areas, guest rooms,
etc. within the hotel. Silver ware is used mainly for tableware, roast
cart, duck press, etc., and they are polished continuously for 24 hours
by four full-time staffs. Concierge services are also provided to meet
the needs of all guests. Thus, this hotel is endeavoring to satisfy the
requirements of any executives, or individuals involved in business
activities.

181, Peachtree Street, NE Atlanta, GA 30303
Phone: 404-659-0400

Design (interior) / Frank Nicholson Inc., Concord, Massachusetts
Opened / April 1984
Scale, number of guest rooms / 25 stories, 454 rooms (incl. 24 suite
　　rooms)
Eating/drinking facilities / The Restaurant, The Cafe, Lobby Lounge
Banquet hall, boardroom / Boardrooms (15) (7,412 sq. ft.)
　　(incl. 2 boardrooms, 2 hospitality suite rooms, and 3 conference
　　suite rooms)

絵画や銀食器類のコレクションが自慢のメインダイニング"The Restaurant"
The main dining hall "The Restaurant" featuring a boastful collection of paintings, silver tableware, etc.

左下・右下/豊富なワインのコレクションをもつ"The Restaurant"のバーとラウンジ
Left bottom, right bottom / The bar and lounge of "The Restaurant" where a rich collection of wine is available.

上・下／"The Cafe"（98席）のバーとレストラン　エレガントな雰囲気のなかでカジュアルに利用できる

Top, bottom / The bar and restaurant of "The Cafe" (98 seats) which can be casually utilized in an elegant atmosphere.

ゴージャスな雰囲気の宴会場ロビー　　　　　The banquet hall's lobby having a gorgeous atmosphere.

リッチなエレベーターホール　　　　　A rich elevator hall.

新しいスタイルのセッティングを備える宴会場ロビー

The banquet hall's lobby equipped with a new-style setting.

VIP客専用フロアにあるクラブ ラウンジ

The club lounge at a floor exclusive for VIP's.

左下・右下／スイートルームは食事用のテーブル席や会議もできるスペースがある
Left bottom, right bottom / The suite room has a space where there are dining table seats, or you can have a meeting.

泉やトロピカル植物を配したアトリウム ロビー

The atrium lobby where a fountain, tropical plants, etc. are arranged.

Sheraton
New Orleans Hotel

500 Canal Street New Orleans, Louisiana 70130
Phone/504-525-2500

Canal street に面した49階建1,200室の外観
The appearance of the 49-storied hotel having 1,200 rooms and facing the Canal Street.

"Lobby Lounge & Bar"はトロピカルムードのなかのカジュアルなバー
"Lobby lounge & bar" is a casual bar in a tropical mood.

広いスペースのロビーとフロント レセプション

シェラトン ニューオーリンズ
アメリカの南部における観光とコンベンション
の都市として知られるニュー オーリンズは1984
年に"ルイジアナ ワールド エキスポ"が開催さ
れ それに向かって11軒の新しいホテルが進出
や増築の計画に加わった。そして 25,000室の
ファースト クラスのホテルやモテルを持つ都市
となった。「シェラトン ニュー オーリンズ」は
1983年春に第一期計画である地上49階建1,200
室を持つ施設を完成した。"人々のためのホテル"
をそのコンセプトにかかげ ゲストルームのカ
ーペットから スタッフのユニフォームに至る
まで 細かな配慮をしたり 高層の近代建築を
意識し 市街の好展望が得られるよう考慮され
居ながらに外の動きがわかるよう工夫され 心
理的な見地まで計算に入れた建築である。
オープン/1983年3月
規模・客室数/地上49階建1,200室（内スイート
　　　85室　ホスピタリティスイート12室）
料飲施設／レストラン＆ラウンジ5
宴会・会議場／会議室41室(53,000sq.-ft.)

SHERATON NEW ORLEANS

"Louisiana World Expo" was held in 1984
in New Orleans, which is known as a city
for tourism and convention in the south of
America. In consideration of the expo, 11
hotels have been included recently in plans
for development and extension, with the
result that New Orleans became a city with
first-class hotels and motels serving 25,000
guest rooms in all. In the spring of 1983,
"Sheraton New Orleans" had completed the
construction of phase 1, with 49 stories
(1,200 rooms). Based on the concept "Hotel
for people," a serious consideration has been
given to all details from the room's carpet
to the staff's uniform. Since this hotel is
a modern high-rise building, it is designed
so that you can appreciate a fine view of
the surrounding streets, and see from your
seat what is happening outside. This hotel
has been built thus by taking into account
any psychological factors.

500, Canal Street, New Orleans, Louisiana
70130
Phone: 504-525-2500

Opened / March 1983
Scale, number of guest rooms / 49 stories,
　　1,200 rooms (incl. 85 suite rooms and 12
　　hospitality rooms)
Eating/drinking facilities / Restaurants &
　　lounges (5)
Banquet hall, boardroom / Boardrooms (41)
　　(53,000 sq. ft.)

The spacious lobby and front reception.

アトリウム ロビーはトロピカルとフレンチ クォーターの雰囲気をとり入れている
The atrium lobby employs both the tropical atmosphere and French quarter's atmosphere.

左下・右下／"Cafe Promenade"（200席）のアトリウムに面したコーナー（右側）とビュッフェのある店内
Left bottom, right bottom / A corner (right side) of "Cafe Promenade" (200 seats) facing the atrium, and the inside with a buffet.

ファイン ダイニング "Saffron" は香料のサフランから名付けられた デザートのディスプレイと店内

レストランとバーへのアプローチ 格調高い家具や敷石のデザインがみられる

(Photo captions)
Top / The fine dining hall "Saffron" has deriv-
ed its name from saffron as a spice. An
inside view with a display of dessert.
Left bottom / The approach to the restaurant
and bar. Dignified furniture, paving stones,
etc. are designed.

４階の大宴会場3,000名収容でき５区分か可能
The large banquet hall at the 4th floor. Capable of accommodating 3,000 persons, it can be divided into four segments.

ティナーシアター レストラン"Rhythms" フレンチ クォーターをテーマとしたミュージカルが売物

2階にあるカクテル ラウンジ"Lagniappe" フレッシュ オイスターやワインも味わえる

(Photo captions)
Top / The dinner theater restaurant "Rhythms" at which musicals using French quarter as a theme are performed.
Bottom / The cocktail lounge "Lagniappe" at the 2nd floor where you can taste fresh oyster, wine, etc.

"River Club" 42階のラウンジを利用できるのは最上部8フロアに宿泊するVIP客たちだけ
"River Club" at the 42nd lounge floor can be used only by VIP's staying at the highest 8 floors.

キングサイズ スイートルーム
A king-size suite room.

支配人からの心配りのプレゼンテーション
A hospitable presentation from the manager.

スイートルームのバスルーム
The bathroom of a suite room.

カナダ政府と共同開発で完成したホテル棟　地上22階建　地下3階　客室505室　下部はビジネスセンター

Pan Pacific Vancouver
HOTEL

300-999 Canada Place Vancouver, British-columbia Canada V6C 3B5
Phone/605-662-8111

(Photo captions)
Top / The hotel building whose construction has been completed under joint development with the Canadian government. 22 stories above and 3 stories under the ground, it has 505 guest rooms. At the lower part is a business center.
Right bottom / The 3rd lobby floor where various eating/drinking facilities are open. The floor at the stairwell part is an office.

各種料飲施設が集まる3階ロビーフロア　吹抜け部分のフロアはオフィス

"バンクーバー国際交通博覧会"(1986年5月)の「カナダ館」(帆を張った建物)が隣接している
Adjacent to the hotel is Canada Pavilion (canvased building) of "Vancouver International Traffic Expo" (May 1986).

アトリウムの3階部分にあるフロント レセプション廻り
The front reception at the 3rd floor level of the atrium.

大宴会場"Crystal Pavilion"のセット風景
A set scene of the large banquet hall "Crystal Pavilion."

150

アトリウムに設けた"Cafe Pacifica"(196席)
"Cafe Pacifica" (196 seats) provided at the atrium.

太平洋とそれを囲む大陸をデザイン化した池がロビーの中央を占める
The lobby's center is occupied by a pond designing the Pacific Ocean and the surrounding continents.

飲茶(ディム サム)のオープンキッチンとカウンター
Dim-Sum's open kitchen and counter.

"Cascade Lounge"(144席)はビュッフェ
"Cascade Lounge" (144 seats) is a buffet.

ファインダイニング"Fivesails"(120席)
The fine dining room "Fivesails" (120 seats).

上・下／メインロビーの専門店街はブティック　宝石　旅行社　美容室　フローリストなどバラエティに富むショップがある

Top, bottom / Along the shopping street at the main lobby are open a variety of shops — boutique, jewelry, travel agent, beauty parlor, florist, etc.

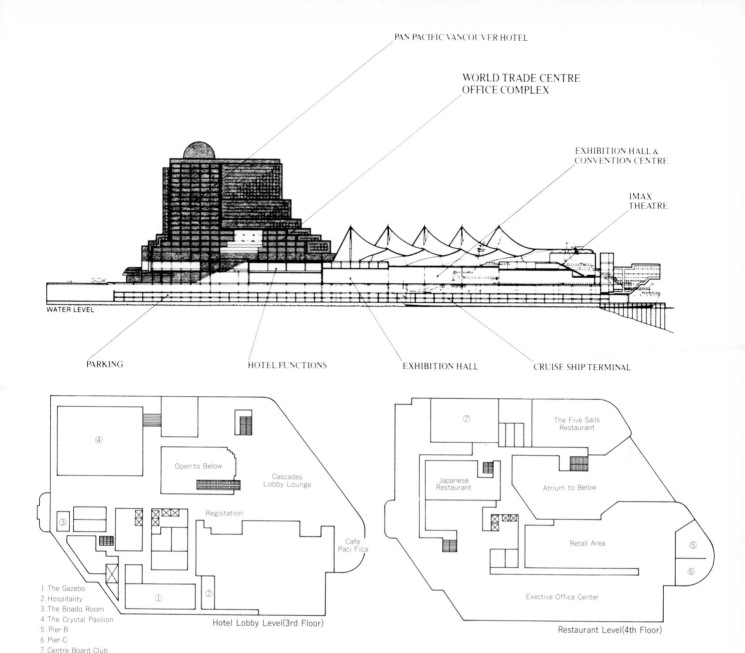

PAN PACIFIC VANCOUVER HOTEL

WORLD TRADE CENTRE
OFFICE COMPLEX

EXHIBITION HALL &
CONVENTION CENTRE

IMAX
THEATRE

WATER LEVEL

PARKING   HOTEL FUNCTIONS   EXHIBITION HALL   CRUISE SHIP TERMINAL

Open to Below

Cascades
Lobby Lounge

Registation

Cafe
Paci Fica

1.The Gazebo
2.Hospitality
3.The Boado Room
4.The Crystal Pavilion
5.Pier-B
6.Pier-C
7.Centre Board Club

Hotel Lobby Level(3rd Floor)

The Five Sails
Restaurant

Japanese
Restaurant

Atrium to Below

Retail Area

Exective Office Center

Restaurant Level(4th Floor)

パン パシフィック バンクーバー ホテル

環太平洋地域を中心「パン パシフィックホテルズ」を展開する「東急ホテ
ルズ インターナショナル」がカナダ・バンクーバーにチェーン11番目に
あたるホテルを開業した。同ホテルは地上22階 地下3階建505室の客室を
持つ規模で "バンクーバー国際交通博覧会(1986年5月2日～10月13日)"
に合わせてオープンし 隣接する「交通博カナダ館」と共に 同地域のラ
ンドマークとなっている。また「ワールド トレードセンター オフィス
コンプレックスビル」との複合建築にもなっている。
レセプションのある3階フロアーには 中央に太平洋とそれを囲む大陸
をデザイン化した池があり その周囲にレストランやラウンジなどが展
開する。客室や これらのパブリックエリアからは外の眺めも良く 好
立地の条件をうまく活かした施設構成になっている。
オープン/1986年4月4日
規模・客室数/地上22階 地下3階建505室(内スペシャルキングルーム28
    室 パーラールーム11室 スイート1室)
料飲施設/5 (テナント店を含む)
宴会・会議場/大宴会場1 (644㎡) 中宴会場4 小宴会場1
その他の施設/ショッピングセンター オフィス階 ヘルスクラブ プー
    ル テニスコート 等

PAN PACIFIC VANCOUVER HOTEL

Tokyu Hotels International, which develops "Pan Pacific Hotels" mainly in the Pan-Pacific zone, has inaugurated their 11th hotel in Vancouver, Canada. With 22 stories above and 3 stories under the ground, and equipped with 505 rooms, it has been opened for the "Vancouver International Traffic Expo" (held from May 2 to October 13, 1986), and at present it serves as a landmark, side by side with the adjacent "Traffic Expo Canada Pavilion." This hotel features also an integrating architecture with the "World Trade Center Office Complex Building."

In the center of the 3rd floor where the reception area is located, there is a pond showing the Pacific Ocean and the surrounding continents, and restaurants, lounges, etc. are arranged around the pond. You can have a fine view of the outside from each guest room, or from any of the public areas. The facilities are arranged thus favorably by taking advantage of their good location.

300-999, Canada Place, Vancouver, British-Columbia, Canada,
V6C 3B5
Phone: 605-662-8111

Opened / April 4, 1986
Scale, number of guest rooms / 22 stories above and 3 stories under
    the ground, 505 rooms (incl. 28 special king rooms, 11 parlor
    rooms and one suite room)
Eating/drinking facilities / 5 (incl. tenant shops)
Banquet hall, boardroom / Large banquet hall (1) (644 m²), Medium-
    size banquet halls (4), Small banquet hall (1)
Other facilities / Shopping center, Office floor, Health club, Pool,
    Tennis court, etc.

テナント出店している"Restaurant Suntory"は寿司バ
ー 鉄板焼 すきやき しゃぶしゃぶ バーラウン
ジ 和室などで構成している

"Restaurant Suntory," which is open as a
tenant, comprises a 'sushi' bar, hot plate dish,
'sukiyaki,' 'shabu shabu,' bar lounge, Japanese
room, etc.

日本人スタッフもいる22階の"パシフィックフロア コンシアージ ラウンジ"
"Pacific Floor Concierge Lounge" at the 22nd floor where Japanese staffs are also working.

"パシフィック スイート"眺望をいかしたレイアウトとリッチな感じのインテリア
"Pacific Suite" featuring the layout to command a fine view and the interior giving a rich impression.

上・下／8階部分の屋上に設けたスポーツ施設　　　　　　　　　　Top, bottom / The sports facilities provided on the roof (8th floor).

3階の屋外プールは軽食サービスの他にテニスコートやヘルスクラブがある
The outdoor pool at the 3rd floor is part of the health club with tennis courts, and there you can have a light meal.

HOTEL
MERIDIEN
NEWPORT BEACH

4500 Mac Arthur Blvd. Newport Beach, CA 92660-2010
Phone/714-476-2001

メインエントランス　右端はレストラン専用
The main entrance. The right side entrance is exclusive for the restaurant.

157

ダイナミックな吹抜け空間の"アトリウム ラウンジ"　　　　　　　　The "Atrium lounge" in the dynamic stairwell space.

3棟構成による440室のユニークな外観
The appearance of the hotel in 3 buildings having 440 rooms.

エントランスホールよりレセプションをみる
The reception area viewed from the entrance hall.

"アトリウム ラウンジ"より"Cafe Fleuri"をみる

"Cafe Fleuri" viewed from "Atrium Lounge."

トロピカルムードの"アトリウム ラウンジ"
"Atrium Lounge" with a tropical mood.

"Cafe Fleuri"のバーコーナー　　The bar corner of "Cafe Fleuri."

宴会場エントランスホールのシャンデリアが印象的   The banquet hall's entrance hall with impressive chandeliers.

ホテル メリディアン ニューポート ビーチ

エールフランスの関連ホテル チェーンとして世界的に展開している「ホテル メリディアン」の51番目にあたるホテル。南カリフォルニアのニューポート地区は　近年多くの会社のヘッドオフィスやショッピングセンターなどの進出により　その規模もだんだんふくらんできており　これらのマーケットを中心にビジネスマン層のニーズに応えているホテルでもある。

その特徴の一つに"LEXAR"と呼ぶ多目的機能を持つ電話を備え　室内の空調やTVのコントロールからホテル内の諸施設をワンタッチで使用可能にするなど　いわゆるインテリジェント機能を持たせている。

フレンチタッチで統一されたインテリアや家具　調度品をはじめ　メインダイニングルームには「ホテル ネグレスコ」のスーパーシェフJacques Maximinによるメニュー指導を導入するなど　ハイプレステージホテルとして注目されている。

オープン/1984年11月1日

規模・客室数/3棟構成440室(内　エグゼクティブ　スイート27室)

料飲施設/レストラン2　バーラウンジ2　ホスピタリティ スイート8

宴会・会議場/大宴会場(7,000sq.-ft.)　会議室11室

その他の施設/プール　ジョギングコース　ヘルスクラブ＆スパ テニスコート

投資額/3,000万ドル

HOTEL MERIDIEN NEWPORT BEACH

This is the 51st "Hotel Meridien" built as part of the hotel chain related to Air France. Newport Beach area in South California has expanded gradually in recent years due to the development in construction of many corporate head offices, shopping centers, etc. Thanks mainly to this growing market, this hotel can satisfy the needs of any businessmen.

One of its features is that this hotel is equipped with multi-function telephones called "LEXAR," or so-called "intelligent" functions from control of indoor air conditioning and TV, to that of various facilities within the hotel, by simply pressing a button.

This hotel is drawing attention as a high prestige hotel by using interior, furniture and utensils that have a French touch, and by offering a main dining's menu prepared under the supervision of super-chef Jacques Maximin, from "Hotel Negresco."

4500, MacArthur Blvd., Newport Beach, CA 92660-2010
Phone: 714-476-2001

Opened / November 1, 1984
Scale, number of guest rooms / Consisting of 3 buildings, 440 rooms (incl. 27 executive suite rooms)
Eating/drinking facilities / Restaurants (2), Bar lounges (2), Hospitality suite rooms (8)
Banquet hall, boardroom / Large banquet hall (7,000 sq. ft.), Boardrooms (11)
Other facilities / Pool, Jogging course, Health club & spa, Tennis court
Total investment / $30 million

大宴会場(7,000sq.-ft.)のディナー セッティング 他に11の会議室と8つのホスピタリティー スイートルームがある
The dinner setting at the large banquet hall (7,000 sq. ft.). There are 11 boardrooms and 8 hospitality suite rooms.

左上・右上／多彩なコーナー設定を施したバー"Trianon"はカジュアルでシックな雰囲気

Left top, right top / The bar "Trianon" featuring varied corners has a casual and chic atmosphere.

"Antoine"のレセプション エリアとレストランへの入口

The reception area of "Antoine" and the entrance to the restaurant.

クリエイティブなフランス料理を提供する"Antoine"は有名なフランスのシェフ・Jacqnes Maximinをスーパーバイザーに起用している
"Antoine," which serves creative French dishes, employs Jacques Maximin, a well-known French chef, as its supervisor.

左下・中下・右下／エレガントな色彩で統一したプレジテンシャル スイートルーム
Left bottom, middle bottom, right bottom / Presidential suite rooms which feature elegant coloring.

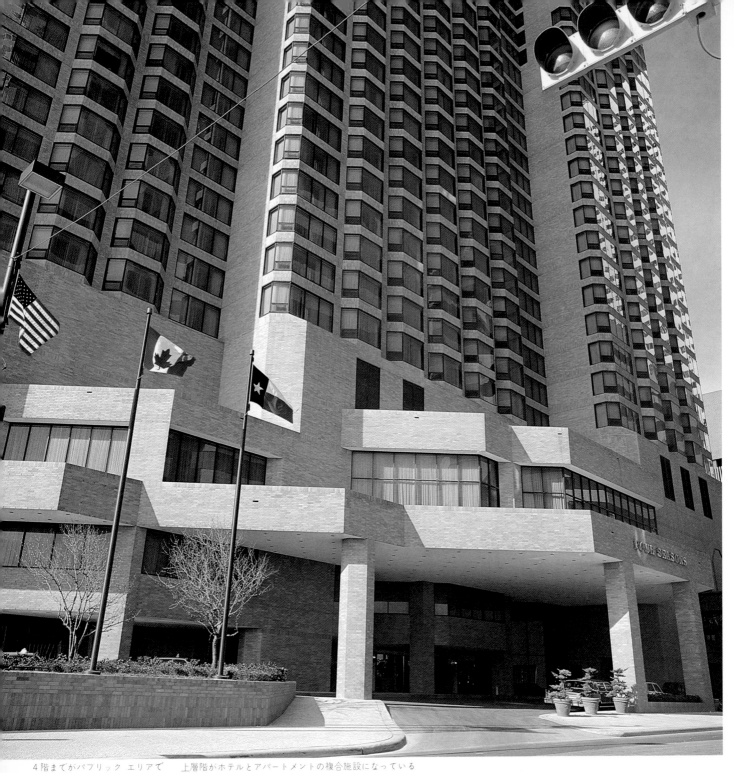

４階までがパブリック エリアで　上層階がホテルとアパートメントの複合施設になっている
Using up to 4 stories as a public space, the higher floors constitute a composite building of hotel and apartment house.

Four Seasons Hotel
HOUSTON CENTER

1300 Lamar Houston, Texas 77010
Phone/713-650-1300

エントランスホール　　　　　　　　　　The entrance hall.

164

広いスペースのロビー　正面がフロント　レセプション
The spacious lobby, with the front reception in your side.

ダウンタウンの再開発としての建てられたホテルと
アパートメント

宴会場ロビーに設けられた公衆電話

(Photo captions)
Top / The hotel and apartment house built
　　as part of the downtown redevelopment
　　program.
Middle / Public telephones provided at the
　　lobby of a banquet hall.
Bottom / The indoor pool attached to athletic
　　facilities.

会議室や宴会場としてレストランの中心部に設けたアトリウム
The atrium provided in the center of areas where boardrooms, banquet halls and restaurants are located.

アスレチック施設に付帯した室内プール

伝統的ヨーロッパスタイルの"Four Seasons Ball Room" イタリア製の大きなシャンデリアが目立つ
"Four Seasons Ballroom" in the traditional European style, featuring large Italian chandeliers.

宴会場とロビーを結ぶグランド ステアーケース（階段）
The grand staircase connecting the banquet hall with the lobby.

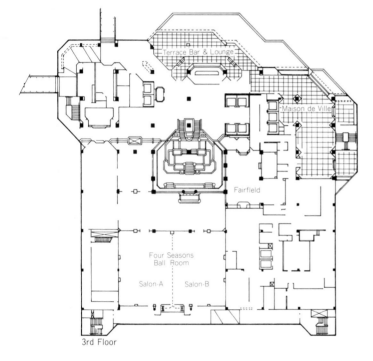

3rd Floor

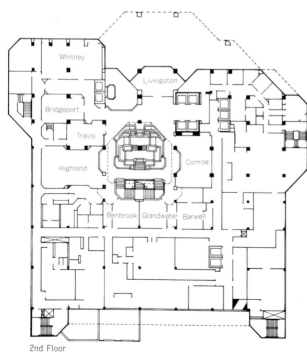

2nd Floor

フォー シーズンズ ホテル ヒューストン センター
「フォー シーズンズ ホテル」はカナダに本拠を持ち カナダ ヨーロッパ アメリカに22のホテルを経営している。代表的なものにニューヨークの「Hotel The Pierre」 シカゴの「The Ritz-Carlton」 サンフランシスコの「The Four Seasons Clift」 ロンドンとトロント ヒューストンに持つ「Inn On The Park」などがある。
ヒューストンのダウンタウンにビジネス 商業地区として33ブロックの新しく開発されている「ヒューストン センター」の一角にホテルと長期リースのレジデンシャル アパートメントから成る30階建の複合建築である。
4階建の1ブロックの広さの建物が土台の部分になっており この建物の上にホテルとアパートメントが建ち上がっている。ミーティングルーム レストラン ラウンジ リクレーション施設 2,700 平方フィートのショップなどパブリックスペースは すべてこの4階建の土台部分の中にある。3階の高い空間に広がる大階段とアトリウムがポーティアム（土台）の中心部にあって ホテルの各パブリックエリアに連絡している。
設計/建築・Clark Darling Downey
　　内装・Armin Trattman & Associates Space Planning and
　　Interior Design
オープン/1982年4月5日
規模・客室数/30階建411室（ホテル）129室（レジデンシャルアパートメント）
料飲施設/The Lobby Lounge & Bar 92席 The Terrace Lounge 72席
　　　Maison de Ville（レストラン）140席
宴会・会議場/大宴会場1（400人収容）ミーティングサロン10室
その他の施設/プール（15フィートのWhirlpool）プールサイド ラウンジ
　　　　屋外リクレーション施設

FOUR SEASONS HOTEL Houston Center

With its headquarters in Canada, "Four Seasons Hotel" chain is managing 22 hotels in Canada, Europe and the U.S., and the representative hotels of this chain include "Hotel The Pierre" in New York, "The Ritz-Carlton" in Chicago, "The Four Seasons Clift" in San Francisco, and "Inn On The Park" in Houston.
This hotel is part of a 30-storied composite building that comprises also long-leased residential apartment houses located at a corner of the "Houston Center" covering 33 blocks which have being newly developed as a downtown business-commercial quarter in Houston. The building stands on a 4-storied foundation covering one block, on which the hotel and apartment houses are located. All public space — meeting rooms, restaurants, lounges, recreation facilities, and 2,700 sq. ft. shops — is included within the 4-storied foundation floors. The large staircase and atrium extending over a 3-storied space are placed in the center of the podium (foundation), leading to each public area in the hotel.

1300, Lamar, Houston, Texas 77010
Phone: 713-650-1300

Design / Architecture: Clark Darling Downey
　　Interior: Armin Trattmann & Associates Space Planning and
　　Interior Design
Opened / April 5, 1982
Scale, number of guest rooms / 30 stories, 411 rooms (hotel),
　　129 rooms (residential apartment house)
Eating/drinking facilities / The lobby lounge & bar (92 seats),
　　The terrace lounge (72 seats),
　　Maison de Ville (restaurant, 40 seats)
Banquet hall, boardroom / Large banquet hall (1, accommodating 400 persons), Meeting salon (10)
Other facilities / Pool (15 feet whirlpool), Poolside lounge, Outdoor recreation facilities

最高級のレストラン"Maison de Ville"（140席）19世紀のベネチアンスタイルのシャンデリアが素晴しい
The highest grade restaurant "Maison de Ville" (140 seats), featuring wonderful Venetian style chandeliers of the 19th century.

"Terrace Lounge"（72席）は一段高くなったテーブル席とカウンターで構成
"Terrace Lounge" (72 seats) consists of elevated table seats and counter.

ロビーレベルにある"Lobby Lounge & Bar"（92席）
"Lobby Lounge & Bar" (92 seats) at the lobby level.

上・下/ゴージャスな雰囲気のプレジデンシャル スイートルーム

Top, bottom / A presidential suite room having a gorgeous atmosphere.

グリーンがいっぱいのアトリウム

The atrium full of green.

ゆったりとしたレイアウトのロビー ラウンジ

The lobby lounge featuring a leisurely layout.

THE WESTIN HOTEL
Tabor Center Denver

1672 Lawrence Street Denver, Colorado 80202
Phone/303-572-9100

再開発が成ったショップとオフィス ホテルのコンプレックス Tabor Center

Tabor Center, a shop-office-hotel complex, that has been favorably redeveloped.

レセプションのカウンター　　　The reception's counter.

コンシアージ デスクと館内案内のTVモニター
The concierge desk and hotel guide TV monitor.

ロビーレヘルのエレヘーターホール
The elevator hall at the lobby level.

ロビーに展開するラウンジ　　　The lounge extending over a lobby.

最大1,000名を収容できる"Continental Ballroom"
"Continental Ballroom" capable of accommodating 1,000 persons at max.

172

ガラス スクリーンで仕切ったメインダイニング"Augusta"（115席）のテーブル席
The table seats of the main dining hall "Augusta" (115 seats) partitioned by glass screens.

"Augusta"に設けたセミ オープンのグリルコーナー
The semi-open grill corner provided at "Augusta."

Top, bottom / Sports/health facilities are provided, such as an athletic sauna room, indoor/outdoor pools, and racket ball court.

上・下/アスレチック　サウナ　屋内・外プール　ラケットボール　コートなどスポーツやヘルスの設備がととのっている

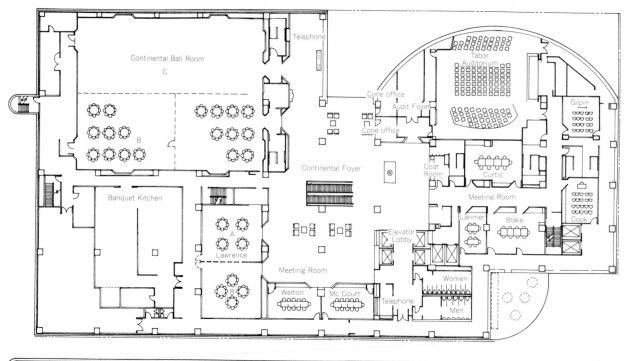

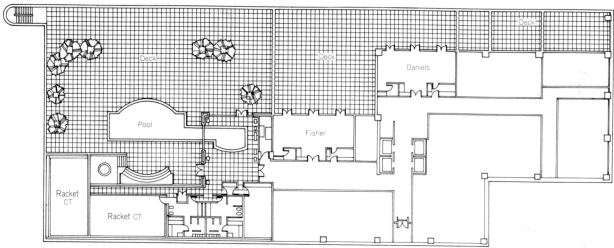

ザ ウエスティン デンバー テイバー センター

ロッキー山脈の束側にあってマイルハイ シティ（標高1,600ｍの都市）と
呼ばれるデンバーは 軍事や産業都市として重要な位置を占めている。
ここに開業した同ホテルは市街地再開発計画として 総事業費 3 億3,000
万ドルが投じられた「テイバー センター コンプレックス」の核施設とし
て ハイクオリティな430室の客室とバラエティに富む14のコンベンショ
ン施設などを備えている。同ホテルとオフィスビルやショッピングセン
ターが結ばれており プレステージの高い「ウエスティン ホテルズ」の
チェーンの中でもハイグレードな施設内容となっている。料飲施設はコ
ンチネンタル料理を中心に フォーマルな雰囲気のダイニングルームと
バーコーナーも付いた カジュアルなスリーミール（３食）レストランや
ロビーラウンジなどで構成している。

オープン/1985年 1 月

規模・客室数/地上19階建430室（内 スイート14室）

料飲施設/メインダイニング1 グリルレストラン1 ロビーラウンジ1

宴会・会議場/宴会場14（大宴会場7,450sq.-ft.1,000名収容含む）

その他の施設/スポーツクラブ（サウナ プール ラケットボールコートな
ど）

THE WESTIN, Tabor Center Denver

Situated in the eastern side of the Rocky Mts., and called "Mile High
City" (a city located at 1,600 m above the sea level), Denver occupies
an important position as a military/industrial city. As central facilities
of "Tabor Center Complex" for which $330 million has been invested
– as part of the urban area redevelopment program – this hotel has
430 high-quality guest rooms, 14 different convention facilities, etc.
It is connected with office buildings and shopping centers. This hotel
is equipped also with high-grade facilities, which are remarkable in
the highly prestigious "Westin Hotels" chain. The eating/drinking
facilities consist of the main dining hall where continental dishes are
mainly served in a formal atmosphere, a casual three-meal restaurant,
lobby lounges, etc.

1672, Lawrence Street, Denver, Colorado 80202
Phone: 303-572-9100

Opened / January 1985
Scale, number of guest rooms / 19 stories, 430 rooms
(incl. 14 suite roms)
Eating/drinking facilities / Main dining room (1), Grille restaurant (1),
Lobby lounge (1)
Banquet hall, boardroom / Banquet hall (14) (incl. 7,450 sq. ft.
large banquet hall, accommodating 1,000 persons)
Other facilities / Sports club (sauna, pool, racket ball court, etc.)

上・下/バーコーナーも付帯のカジュアルレストラン"Tabor Grill"（125席）

Top, bottom / The casual restaurant "Tabor Grill" (125 seats), with a bar corner attached.

上・下/プレジデンシャル スイートルーム ウェット
バーも設けゴージャスな雰囲気で構成している
Top, bottom / A presidential suite room, having a gorgeous atmosphere with a wet bar.

コンテンポラリーのデザインが特徴のエントランスホール

The entrance hall featuring a contemporary design.

MORGANS

237 Madison Avenue New York, N.Y. 10016
Phone / 212-686-0300

This hotel building came into being by fully redecorating "The Duane Hotel" which was built in 1929.

1929年に"The Duane Hotel"として建てられたものを全面改装したもの ホテル名も見当らない外観

フロアデザインが強い印象を与えるエレベーターホール　　　　　　　　　The elevator hall with a very impressive floor design.

モーガンズ

ニューヨークの「Studio 54」のオーナーであった　スティーブ ルーベイル (Steve Rubell)とイアン シュレイガー(Ian Schrager)がつくった“ブティック ホテル”である。これまでのホテルのステレオタイプをうち破り　家庭らしさを表現するというコンセプトのホテルだ。オーナーの美意識や価値観が　ファッション ブティックのように一貫して表現されたホテルである。パーソナリティを前面にうち出した各種サービスは　アメリカのハイソサエティの客層に大きな衝撃を与えている。モーガンズという名前は　この建物が銀行王のJ.P.モーガンのかつての屋敷でありまた近く博物館「モーガン ライブラリー」を見下ろす位置にあるところから名づけられている。24時間ルーム サービスや宿泊客全ての好みをコンピューターに登録し「ゲスト ヒストリーズ」を試みたり　全室異なるインテリアデザインを採用するなど　きめの細かなサービスをしているのも同ホテルの特徴。50年以上も前に建てられた古いホテルを約1年かけて全面改装したものである。

オープン/1984年10月1日

規模・客室数/154室(スイート28 ロストスイート6　ペントハウス1を
　　　含む)　料飲施設/バー1　レストラン1

MORGANS

A "boutique hotel" created by Steve Rubell, former owner of the well-known "Studio 54" in New York, and Ian Schrager. Breaking the stereotype of conventional hotel images, this hotel presents the concept of a homely atmosphere. Thus, the owner's aesthetic and value senses are fully expressed in this hotel as in a fashion boutique. Various services featuring personality are greatly influencing the American high-society people. The name "Morgans" comes from the fact that the building was the former residence of J.P. Morgan, a bank magnate, and it is situated at a place overlooking the neighboring museum "Morgan Library." The hotel provides also a 24-hour room service that adopts "guest histories" in which the tastes and needs of all guests are stored in computer, and its interior design changes from room to room, offering thus high quality services.

237, Madison Avenue, New York, N.Y. 10016
Phone: 212-686-0300

Opened / October 1, 1984

白と黒のパターンを活かした客室

低いベッドをもつコンテンポラリー感覚のヘッド
ルーム

シースルーでバスルームとトイレが仕切られ
ている

(Photo captions)
Top / A guest room featuring white-black
　　pattern.
Middle / A bedroom having a contemporary
　　feeling with a low bed.
Bottom / The bathroom and toilet are par-
　　titioned by see-through glass.

格調あるエントランスホール　　　　　　The dignified entrance hall.

地下1階にあるレストランのユニークなテーブル席レイアウト
The unique layout of table seats in a restaurant at the 1st basement.

ブルックリンにある"River Cafe"の名シェフが料理を手がけるレストラン
The restaurant serving dishes at the instructions of master chef of "River Café" in Brooklyn.

併設したバーよりダイニング エリアをみる
The dining room viewed from the attached bar.

シンプルでモダンな感じのバーコーナー
The bar corner having a simple, modern feeling.

181

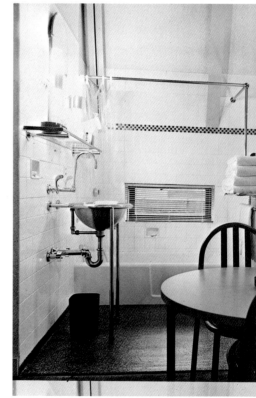

左上・左下・中上・中下/これまでのホテル界の常識
や伝統を打ち破り　斬新なデザインを導入した客
室"カテドラル"　聖堂のイメージで構成した部屋
バスルームにテーブルを持ち込む発想がユニーク

(Photo captions)
Left top, left middle, middle top, middle bottom / Breaking the common sense and tradi-
tion of conventional hotel business, the
guest room "Cathedra" employs a brand-
new design. It consists of a room featuring
an image of cathedral, a bathroom with a
table – unique idea – and other facilities.

右上・右下/螺旋階段を配したペントハウスはハイ
レベルの構成で　2階がリビングとベッドルーム
になっている

(Photo captions)
Right top, right bottom / The penthouse with
a spiral staircase is of bi-level structure,
and the 2nd floor constitutes the living
room and bedroom.

上・左下／ビスケイ湾を望むココナッツグローフの高級ショッピングセンター コンプレックスにある外観

Mayfair House

3000 Florida Avenue Coconut Grove, Miami Florida 33133
Phone/305-441-0600

Top, right bottom / The appearance of the hotel which stands in a coconut grove high-grade shopping center complex overlooking the Bay of Biscay.

中庭を囲む形で客室がレイアウトされた"水と緑と光"をテーマにしたホテル

屋上にある"The Rooftop Garden Bar & Pool"
"The Rooftop Garden Bar & Pool" on the roof.

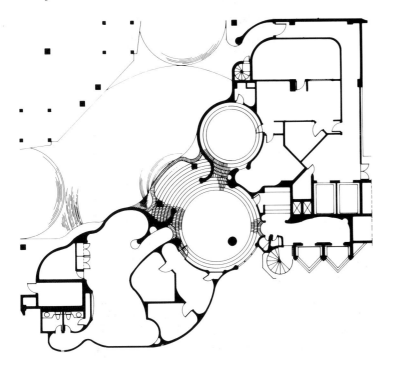

メイフェア ハウス

フロリダ州マイアミのココナッツ グローブに
高級ショッピングセンターと複合するこのホテ
ルは 最近急増している"ブティック ホテル"の
一つとして大変人気がある。数少ない客室なが
ら豪華で個性的な施設や設備を有し パーソナ
ルタッチのサービスを提供している。マホガニ
ー製家具 ホットタブ付のバルコニーを設けた
ラグジュアリィな客室 会員制のレストラン
クラブ バー リゾート施設など 随所に新し
いアイデアを盛り込んでいる。場所柄ハネーム
ーンなどにもよく利用されている同ホテルは
"ブティック ホテル"によるリファーラル グル
ープ「スモール ラグジュアリィ ホテルズ(略称
SLH)」の他「ザ リーディング ホテルズ オブ
ザ ワールド(略称LHW)」の加盟ホテルでもあ
る。

オープン/1985年春
規模・客室数/1810室(全室バルコニー 屋外ホ
　　ットタブ付)
料飲施設/ 3　Mayfair Grill. Tiffany Lounge.
　　Ensign Bitter's.(プライベート クラブ)
その他の施設/ルーフトップガーデン＆プール

Top / The hotel pursuing "water, green and light" as a theme, with guest rooms surrounding the courtyard.

MAYFAIR HOUSE

Situated at Coconut Grove, Miami, Florida, and connected with à high-grade shopping center, this hotel is very popular as one of the "boutique hotels" which are now increasing in number at a high rate. Although in limited number, the guest rooms are equipped with gorgeous and individual facilities, furniture, etc., and are offering personal services. Mahogany furniture, luxurious guest rooms provided with a balcony having a hot tub, a membership restaurant, club, bar, resort facilities, etc. — new ideas are thus incorporated in the design of this hotel whose location is such that it is often selected by honeymooners. It is a member of "Small Luxury Hotels" (SLH), a group of "boutique hotels" and also a member of "The Leading Hotels of The World" (LHW).

3000, Florida Avenue, Coconut Grove,
Miami, Florida 33133
Phone: 305-441-0000

Opened / Spring, 1985
Scale, number of guest rooms / 1,810 rooms
　　(all with a balcony and outdoor hot tub)
Eating/drinking facilities / Mayfair grill,
　　Tiffany lounge, Ensign Bitter's (private
　　club)
Other facilities / Rooftop garden & pool

中庭に面した客室へのシースルー エレベーター

エントランスホール

ロビー近くの"Tiffany Lounge" コーヒーとカクテルを
提供する

芸術的にも評価の高いロビーとコンシアージ デスク
The lobby which is highly reputed artistically, and the concierge desk.

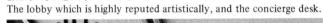

(Photo captions)
Top / The see-through elevator to guest rooms
　　that face the courtyard.
Middle / The entrance hall.
Bottom / "Tiffany Lounge" near the lobby
　　serves coffee and cocktail.

デザインタイルを配した客室フロアの通路
An aisle at the guest room floor where design tiles are arranged.

"Mayfair Grill"のテラスサイドにある"オーキッド ルーム"貝を形どった椅子やステンドグラス
"Oaked Room" on the terrace side of "Mayfair Grill," featuring the shell-shaped chairs and stained glass.

"Mayfair Grill & Bar"はヨーロッパと東洋のアートが採り入れられている
"Mayfair Grill Bar" employs the European and Oriental art works.

"The Rooftop Garden Bar"は軽食とカクテルを提供

"The Rooftop Garden Bar" serves light meals and cocktail.

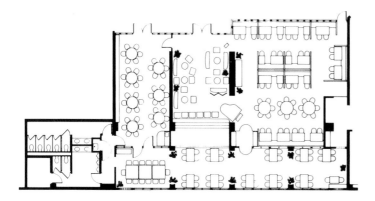

上・左下／プライベート クラブ"En ign Bitter's" はラウンジとダイニングルームから構成している

Top, left bottom / The private club "En ign Bitter's" consists of a lounge and dining room.

上・下／各室ごとにデザインが異なっているのがこのブティックホテルの特徴

Top, Bottom/This boutique hotel features design differing from room to room.

Y字型の建物は28階 1,503室と巨大なコンベンション施設及びリゾート施設で構成している
Y-shaped building, 28-storied, has 1,503 guest rooms, huge convention facilities and resort facilities.

MARRIOTT'S
Orlando World Center
RESORT AND CONVENTION CENTER

World Center Drive Orlando, Florida 32821
Phone/305-239-4200

階段上に延びる両翼状の外観はホテルの正面
The two-winged appearance extending over the staircase shows the front side of the hotel.

メインエントランスのホール

アトリウムロビーよりフロント レセプションをみる

"The Lobby Shop"

200エーカー（約25万坪）の敷地内に Joe Lee が設計したゴルフ場をはじめテニス場　プールがある
Over the 200 acres of site extend golf links designed by Jon Lee, tennis courts and pools.

両翼の中央部にあるアトリウム ロビー　　　　The atrium lobby in the center of two wings.

(Photo captions)
Top / The main entrance hall.
Middle / The front reception viewed from the
　　atrium's lobby.
Bottom / "The Lobby Shop."

建物に変化をつけ楽しさを表現している　グリーンの屋根はレストラン"Mikado"
The building employs varied, amusing expressions.　The restaurant "Mikado" is green-roofed.

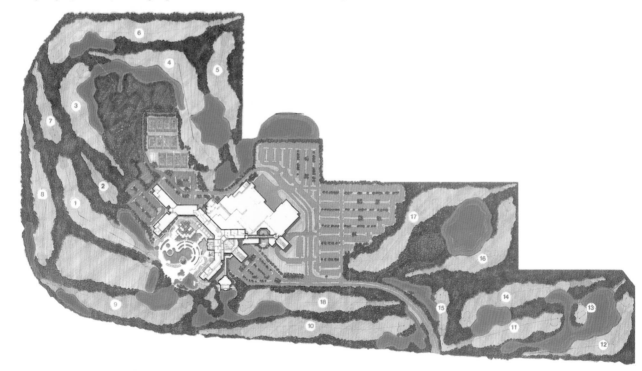

マリオット　オーランド　ワールド　センター

フロリダ州オーランドは「ディズニーワールド」や「エプコットセンター」などで知られる東部のレジャーランドで有名であるが　ここを中心に最近多くのホテルが進出を続けている。2億5,000万ドルを投資し　4年間を費やした計画と工事の後にオープンした「マリオット」は　オーランドで最大級といわれるコンベンション施設や200エーカーの敷地内にゴルフ場　夜間照明付のテニスコート12面2,000台収容の駐車場　ラグーン形のプールと熱帯樹　滝などを配したトロピカルガーデンと28階建1,503室の巨大ホテル部分などで構成している。料飲施設は10ヵ所あって　ファーストフード店からプールサイドのバーラウンジなどが　完備している典型的なリゾート型コンベンションホテルである。Y字型の階段状に延びるホテル建築の雄姿がフロリダの青い空に映え　ここを訪れる人々はリゾートライフを十分にエンジョイできる。

オープン/1986年5月15日

規模・客室数/28階建1,503室(内　スイート101室)

料飲施設/10(ルームサービス　バンケット　レストランを含む。1
　　　日の供給量は20,000食まで可能)

宴会・会議場/グランドボールルーム(38,675sq.-ft.) クリスタルボー
　　　ルルーム(40,740sq.-ft.) 会議室46室

その他の施設/プール4　スパ5　ヘルス　エクササイズ　クラブ
　　　テニスコート(夜間照明付)12面　ゴルフコース18ホール　ゴ
　　　ルフクラブ　バー＆グリル　ギフトショップ3

MARRIOTT'S Orlando World Center

Orlando, Florida, is famous as a leisure land in the East, where "Disney World," "Epcot Center," etc. can be found. Recently, many hotels have been constructed in this area.

With $250 million invested, and 4 years spent in planning and construction, "Marriott" is equipped with one of Orlando's largest convention facilities, golf links, 12 tennis courts, parking place to accommodate 2,000 cars, a tropical garden with a lagoon-shape pool, tropical trees, waterfall, etc., and 25-storied, huge hotel with 1,503 rooms over 200 acres of site. There are 10 eating/drinking facilities, ranging from fast food shops to a poolside bar lounge. "Marriott" can be considered as a typical resort convention hotel. The hotel building looking like a Y-shaped staircase is shining magnificently in the blue sky of Florida, and visitors can fully enjoy a resort life.

World Center Drive, Orland, Florida 32821
Phone: 305-239-4200

Opened / May 15, 1986
Scale, number of guests / 27 stories, 1,503 rooms
　　　(incl. 101 suite rooms)
Eating/drinking facilities / 10 (incl. room service, banquet halls
　　　and restaurants), 20,000 meals a day can be supplied.
Banquet hall, boardroom / Grand ballroom (38,675 sq. ft.),
　　　Crystal ballroom (40,740 sq. ft.), Boardroom (46)
Other facilities / Pool (4), Spa (5), Health exercise club,
　　　Tennis courts (12) with night lighting, Golf course (18 holes),
　　　Golf club, Bar & grille, Gift shop (3)

上・下/アトリウムにあるバーラウンジ"The Pagoda Lounge"ピアノを聞きながら　ラグーンやプール　滝を眺めて楽しむ

Top, bottom / The bar lounge "The Pagoda Lounge" at the atrium. While listening to piano, you can enjoy the views of lagoon, pool and waterfall.

ファイン ダイニングルーム"Regent Court" ディナーのみでシーフード ステーキ ダックを提供する
The fine dining room "Regent Court" serving dinner alone of seafood, steak and duck.

日本庭園のある鉄板焼きステーキのレストラン"Mikado House"（112席）
The hot plate steak restaurant "Mikado Steak House" having a Japanese garden.

上・下／ファースト フード "Stachio's" はフライド チキン　ハンバーガー　ピザなどを提供している

Top, bottom / The fast food "Stachio's" serves fried chicken, hamburger, pizza, etc.

上・下/モロッコ風のカジュアル レストラン "Garden Terrace"（500席） ビュッフェ コーナーもある

Top, bottom / The Moroccan casual restaurant "Garden Terrace" (150 seats), provided also with a buffet corner.

プールサイドのカフェテリア"The Palms"朝食とランチを提供する
The poolside cafeteria "The Palms," serving breakfast and lunch.

ビデオを楽しみながらダンスができるナイト　スポット"Overtures"
The night spot "Overtures" where you can dance while enjoyihg video.

コンシアージ レベルの客室（100室）に宿泊する客専用の"Club Lounge"

会議　宴会場のスカイライトをとり入れたコリドー

ゴルフ客の朝食とランチを提供する"Golf Club & Grill"

レセプションの準備もととのった大宴会場

(Photo captions)
Left top / The corridor employing skylight of boardrooms and banquet halls.
Left bottom / The large banquet hall where preparations for a reception are over.
Right top / The "Club Lounge" exclusive for guests who stay at guest rooms (100) at the concierge level.
Right bottom / The "Golf Club & Grill" serving breakfast and lunch to golf guests.

上・下/最上階の28階にある広く　リッチなスイートルーム"International Presidential Suite"

Top, bottom / The spacious, rich suite room "International Presidential Suite" at the highest 28th floor.

200

"Dana Point Pool"のプールサイドよりメインビルディングのテラス付き"The Cafe"をみる
The terraced "The Café" in the main building viewed from the poolside of "Dana Point Pool."

THE RITZ-CARLTON
LAGUNA NIGUEL

33533 Shoreline Drive Laguna Niguel, CA 92677
Phone/714-240-2000

"The Cafe"のテラスよりプール及びプールバーをみる
The pool and pool bar viewed from the terrace of "The Café."

"Monarch Bay" とそのウイング棟及び"Monarch Bay Pool"をみる
"Monarch Bay" and its wing building, and "Monarch Bay Pool."

地中海風のホテルの外観
The appearance of the Mediterranean hotel.

本館よりプールサイドへのコートヤードにある泉
A fountain along the courtyard leading from the main building to the poolside.

宴会場へ通じる階段　The staircase leading to a banquet hall.

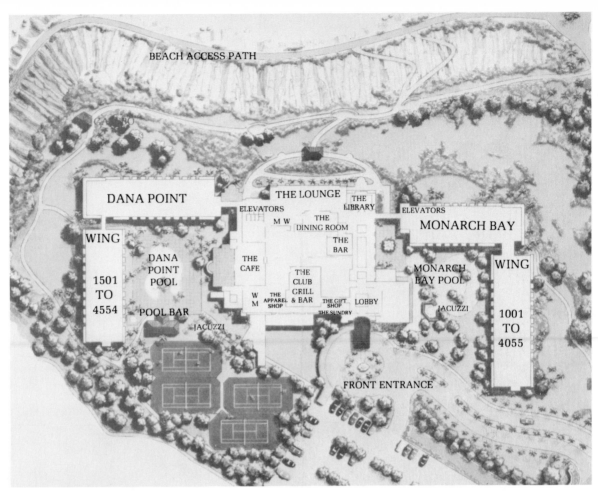

BEACH ACCESS PATH

DANA POINT

THE LOUNGE

THE LIBRARY

ELEVATORS
M W

THE DINING ROOM

ELEVATORS

MONARCH BAY

WING

THE BAR

DANA POINT POOL

THE CAFE

1501 TO 4554

THE CLUB GRILL & BAR

MONARCH BAY POOL

WING

W M

THE APPAREL SHOP

THE GIFT SHOP

LOBBY

1001 TO 4055

POOL BAR

THE SUNDRY

JACUZZI

JACUZZI

FRONT ENTRANCE

ザ リッツ カールトン ラグナ ニゲル

ライオンのロゴで知られる高級ホテル「リッツ カールトン」は
アメリカのビル業界大手W.B.Johnson Properties社の子会社で
ボストン アトランタ フロリダなどにクラシックで豪華なホ
テルを展開する「Ritz-Carlton Hotels Co.」が経営している。カ
リフォルニア州のラグナ ニゲルに開業したこの超デラックス
リゾートホテルは 太平洋を一望する断崖の上に建つ 地中海
風建築で 地上4階建393室の客室と7ヵ所のレストラン バ
ーなどの他にゴルフコース テニスコート フィットネスセン
ター プールなどで構成している。客室からパブリックエリア
に至るまで すばらしいアートコレクションが飾られ これら
は18・19世紀のアメリカとヨーロッパの作品が主だ。「The Leading Hotels of The World(略称LHW)」のメンバーホテルと同
時に1987年には"Mobil Travel Guide"の5つ星に選ばれるなど
大変評価と名声の高いホテルである。

オープン/1984年8月

規模・客室数/4階建393室(内 スイート31室)

料飲施設/7 (The Dining Room. The Lounge. The Pool Bar
など)

宴会・会議場/14室(The Ritz-Carlton Ballroom 9,207sq.-ft. な
ど トータル16,300sq.-ft.)

その他の施設/ゴルフコース 18ホール テニスコート 4面 フ
ィットネスセンター プール2 バレーボールコート

THE RITZ-CARLTON, Laguna Niguel

Known for its lion logo, the hgh-class hotel "The Ritz-Carlton" is operated by "Ritz-Carlton Hotels Co.," a subsidiary of W. B. Johnson Properties, a major building constructor in the U.S., developing classic, gorgeous hotels in Boston, Atlanta, Florida, etc.

Built in Laguna Niguel, California, this super deluxe resort hotel features a Mediterranean style architecture, while standing on a cliff that overlooks the Pacific Ocean. It has 393 guest rooms on 4 stories, equipped with restaurants and bars at 7 locations, golf links, tennis courts, fitness center, pools, etc. Both guest rooms and public areas are decorated with wonderful art works, including American and European works of the 18th and 19th centuries. This hotel is a member of "The Leading Hotels of The World" (LHW), and it has been nominated as Five Stars in 1987 by the "Mobil Travel Guide." It is a highly reputed and celebrated hotel.

33533, Shoreline Drive, Laguna Niguel, CA 92677
Phone: 714-240-2000

Opened / August, 1984
Scale, number of guest rooms / 4 stories, 393 rooms
   (incl. 31 suite rooms)
Eating/drinking facilities / 7 (The Dining Room, The Lounge,
   The Pool Bar, etc.)
Banquet hall, boardroom / 14 (The Ritz-Carlton Ballroom,
   9,207 sq. ft., etc., totaling 16,300 sq. ft.)
Other facilities / Golf course (18 holes), Tennis court (4),
   Fitness center, Pool (2), Volleyball court

パブリック エリアには18〜19世紀の欧米美術品が飾られ　まさに美術館のようだ
At the public area are displayed American and European art works of the 18th to 19th century, just looking like an art museum.

エレガントな雰囲気のフロント
The front with an elegant atmosphere.

海側に面して眺望のよい"The Lounge"
"The Lounge" in the sea side, commanding a fine view.

メイン ダイニング"The Dining Room"（85席）はパーソナル タッチのエレガントな雰囲気
The main dining room "The Dining Room" (85 seats) has a personal, elegant atmosphere.

宴会場とロビーを結ぶ階段
The staircase connecting the banquet hall with the lobby.

プールサイドに面したカジュアル レストラン "The Cafe"（200席）

The casual restaurant "The Cafe" (200 seats) facing the poolside.

"The Cafe"はテラス コーナーもあって開放的

"The Cafe" features an open atmosphere, with a terrace corner.

"Ritz-Carlton Club"のコンシアージ デスク

The concierge desk of "Ritz-Carlton Club."

THE BAR

上・左下／"The Dining Room"に隣接する"The Bar"は重厚な雰囲気のなかにピアノのソフトな音楽が流れる

Top, left bottom / "The Bar" adjacent to "The Dining Room." In a dignified atmosphere, soft piano music is on air.

上・下／素晴しい絵画やワインのコレクションがあるサパークラブ"The Club Grill & Bar" 音楽とダンスも楽しめる

Top, bottom / At "The Club Grill & Bar," a supper club featuring wonderful collections of paintings and wine, you can enjoy music and dance.

"The Cafe"のテラス席　プールを見おろすダイニングは開放的な雰囲気
The terrace seats at "The Cafe." The dining room overlooking the pool has an open atmosphere.

393室ある客室のうち31室がスイート ルーム "Honor Bar" と呼ぶ客室備え付けのバーや豪華なアメニティ イタリアン大理石のバスルームなどサービスが行き 届いている

Of 393 guest rooms, 31 are suite rooms. They feature attentive service equipment, such as "Honor Bar" attached to the guest room, amenities, and the Italian marbled bathroom.

４階の高さのアトリウムにレストラン　バー　宴会場などを設けている　下は宴会場への出入口
The atrium, 4 stories high, is provided with restaurants, bars, banquet halls, etc. shown below is an entrance to the banquet halls.

HYATT REGENCY
OAKLAND

10013 Broadway Oakland, CA 94607
Phone/415-893-1234

コンベンションセンターとジョイントしたホテル（後方の高層）
The hotel (high-rise building at the back) joined with the convention center.

21階建て 488室のホテルの外観
The appearance of the 21-storied hotel, with 488 guest rooms.

ロビー廻り　　　　　　　　　　　　　　　　　　　Around the lobby.

スカイライトの入るアトリウムより宴会　会議室を結ぶ通路
An aisle connecting the skylighted atrium with the banquet hall and boardroom area.

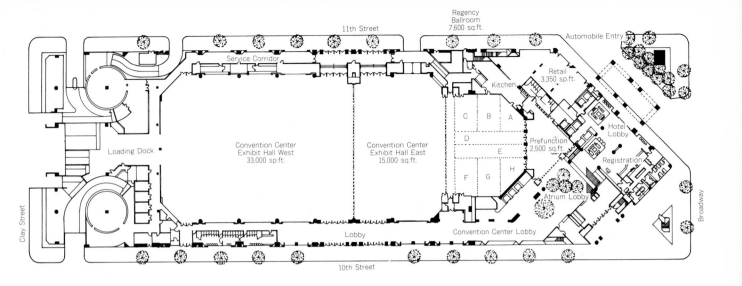

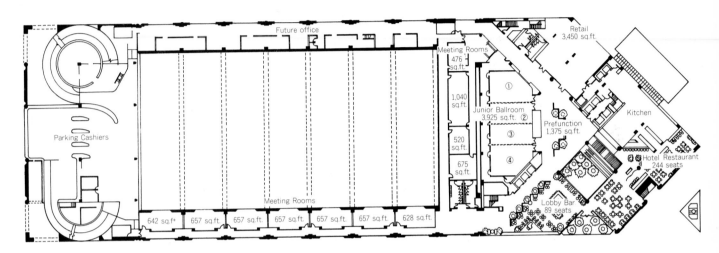

ハイアット リージェンシィ オークランド

サンフランシスコの対岸にあるオークランド市にホテルとコンベンションセンターをジョイントした大規模なプロジェクトが完成した。ダウンタウンの再開発の核として7,700万ドルが投じられた。そのうち4,400万ドルをかけたホテルは488室の中規模ではあるが 15,000sq.-ft. を占める会議室と宴会場をジョイントし 外壁には天候によって色が変化する "Pleke-Therm Sandstone Panel"のシステムを採用し ユニークな建物となった。
4階建のスカイライトを導入したアトリウムを設け その周囲にレストランやバーコーナーを置き グリーンのプラントなども加わって温かさと親しさを感じさせる館内の雰囲気づくりとしている。
オープン/1981年9月
規模・客室数/21階建488室(内　スイート19室)
料飲施設/3（Regency Cafe. Breeze's. A. J. Topper's.）
宴会・会議場/The Regency Ballroom(10,000sq.-ft.) The Junior Ballroom(3,900sq.-ft.) 会議室2
その他の施設/Oakland Convention Center(47,000sp.-ft.) オール アルミニウム プール

HYATT REGENCY OAKLAND

In Oakland City on the opposite bank of San Francisco, a large-scale project has been completed by joining the hotel and convention center, through an investment of $77 million, and it represents the core of the downtown redevelopment program. Of the total, $44 million has been invested in the hotel which is of medium size with 488 rooms, but is designed to cover 15,000 sq. ft. of conference hall and banquet hall. The outer wall has been constructed with the "Pleke-Therm Sandstone Panel" system that changes color according to weather, giving thus the feature of a unique building. An atrium, 4 stories high, is provided with skylight, around which are arranged restaurants, bar corners, etc. Green plants, etc. give the feeling of a warm, familiar atmosphere in the building.

1001, Broadway, Oakland, CA 94607
Phone: 415-893-1234

Opened / September, 1981
Scale, number of guest rooms / 21 stories, 488 rooms
(incl. 19 suite rooms)
Eating/drinking facilities / 3 (Regency Café, Breeze's, A. J. Topper's)
Banquet hall, boardroom / The Regency Ballroom (10,000 sq. ft.),
The Junior Ballroom (3,900 sq. ft.) Boardroom (2)
Other facilities / Oakland Convention Center (47,000 sq. ft.),
All aluminum pool

最上階に設けられた"A. J. Topper's Bar"のバーカウンター

The bar counter of "A. J. Topper's Bar" provided at the highest floor.

左下・右下／"The Regency Cafe"のレセプションとカジュアルなダイニング エリア

Left bottom, right bottom / The reception and casual dining area of "The Regency Café."

ゆったりとしたアームチェアーを配した"A.J. Topper's Bar"のラウンジ　　　　The lounge of "A. J. Topper's Bar" with comfortable armchairs.

2階にあるロビーバー"Breezes"
The lobby bar "Breezes" at the 2nd floor.

A.J. Topper's"のレストラン　　　　"A. J. Topper's" restaurant.

アトリウムに面した"Breezes"

"Breezes" facing the atrium.

上・下／エグゼクティブ スイートルームのリビングとベッドルーム

Top, bottom / The living room and bedroom of an executive suite room.

高級リゾート地マリーナ デル レイ
Marina del Rey — high-class resort.

エレガントな色彩のロビー ラウンジ　　The elegantly colored lobby lounge.

流線型の外観　　The streamlined appearance.

エントランス近くの屋外プール
The outdoor pool near the entrance.

格調あるフロント レセプション　　The dignified front reception.

4100 Admiralty Way Marina del Rey, CA 90292
Phone/213-822-1010

エレベーターホール　　The elevator hall.

ロビーにあるバーコーナー　左奥はレストラン"Stones"の入口

The bar corner at a lobby.　At an inner left part is the restaurant's entrance.

左下・右下/開放的なテラス風カフェ"La Cour"（170席）
Left bottom, right bottom / The open terrace-type café "La Cour" (170 seats).

上・下/広いスペースの宴会場フロア　大宴会場は6,000sq.-ft. 他に会議室が5室(合計3,000sq.-ft.)ある

Top, bottom / The spacious banquet hall floor. The large banquet hall is 6,000 sq. ft. wide. There also are 5 boardrooms (totaling 3,000 sq. ft. wide).

眺望が素晴らしい"Skyfan Lounge"は最上階にあってL字型のレイアウト
"Skyfan Lounge," commanding a fine view, is located at the highest floor, and features L-shaped layout.

マリナ ビーチ ホテル
ロサンゼルス国際空港より約8km北にあって　ビジネスとリゾートで発
展を続けるマリーナ デル レイにオープンした。当地を中心に不動産経
営をしているReal Property Management, Ins.(RPM)社が持つ「Marina
Hotels」の最も新しい3番目のホテルである。
波が動いているような形の外観には　明るいサーモン色を用い　内部は
クラシカルな雰囲気を保ちながら　ブルーグリーン　ピーチ　クリーム
などのパステル調の色彩と　ブラスやガラス製品でアクセントをつけて
いる。場所柄"カジュアル エレガンス"をテーマにしており　高級リゾー
トとビジネスの多目的利用ホテルとして好評である。このグループは
1989年中に　さらに300室の「マリーナ プラザ ホテル」の開業を予定し
ている。
オープン/1986年春
規模・客室数/地上9階建300室(内スイート38室)
料飲施設/4：Stones 80席 La Cour(テラスカフェ)170席 Lobby Lounge.
　　　Skyfan Lounge
宴会・会議場/Grand Ballroom(6,000sq.-ft.) 会議室5 (合計3,000sq.-ft.)
その他の施設/プール　ボートクルーズ
投資額/5,600万ドル

MARINA BEACH HOTEL

This hotel has been built in Marina del Rey, about 8 km north of Los
Angeles International Airport, an area that is developing now with
business and resort facilities. It is the 3rd, latest hotel of "Marina
Hotels" owned by Real Property Management, Inc. (RPM) which is
engaged in real estate operation mainly in this area.
The appearance of this building gives the image of moving waves, and
a bright salmon color has been used. The inside employs pastel colors
– blue green, peach, cream, etc. – while maintaining a classical atmosphere, through the use of brass or glass ware. In consideration of the
area's features, this hotel features the "casual elegance" as its theme,
and is highly reputed as a multi-purpose facility for high-class resort,
business, etc.
This group is planning to open "Marina Plaza Hotel" with 300 guest
rooms within 1989.

4100, Admiralty Way, Marina del Rey, CA 90292
Phone: 213-822-1010

Opened / Spring, 1986
Scale, number of guest rooms / 9 stories, 300 guest rooms
　　(incl. 38 suite rooms)
Eating/drinking facilities / 4; Stones (80 seats), La Cour (terrace café,
　　170 seats), Lobby cocktail lounge, Skyfan lounge
Banquet hall, boardroom / Grand Ballroom (6,000 sq. ft.),
　　Boardroom (5, totaling 3,000 sq. ft.)
Other facilities / Pool, Boat cruise
Total investment / $56 million

"Skyfan Lounge" ペントハウス エンターテイメント ラウンジとしてダンスや音楽が楽しめる
"Skyfan Lounge" where, as a penthouse entertainment lounge, you can enjoy dance and music.

スペシャリティー レストラン
"Stones"（80席）の料理は新し
いスタイルのカリフォルニア
料理

The specialty restaurant "Stones" (80 seats) serves new-type Californian dishes.

テーマカラーのピーチとクリーム色を配したダイニングルーム
The dining room featuring arrangement of theme colors – peach and cream.

左下・右上・右中・右下/プレジデンシャル スイートルーム
Left bottom, right top, right middle, right bottom / A presidential suite room.

このホテルの自慢ともいえる"Signature Room"には政界・財界をはじめ有名人のサイン コレクションがある
At "Signature Room," which is the pride of this hotel, is a collection of signatures of celebrities in the political and financial circles, etc.

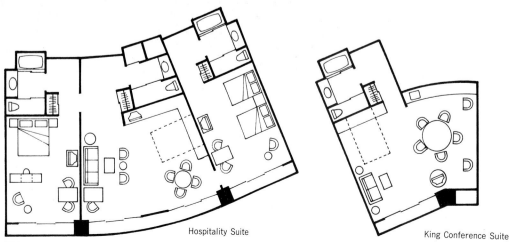

Hospitality Suite

King Conference Suite

ゴルフコースやヘルスクラブなどを付帯するビジネスとリゾートの多目的ホテル
The multi-purpose business and resort hotel, provided with golf courses, health club, etc.

Radisson Plaza Hotel
and Golf Course

1400 Parkview Avenue Manhattan Beach, CA 90266
Phone／213-546-7511

ロビー アトリウム   The lobby atrium.

ピアノ演奏が流れる"Lobby Bar"

"Lobby Bar" where piano music is on air.

エントランス ホールよりフロント レセプション方向をみる
The front reception area viewed from the entrance hall.

左頁下・上/バーコーナーもあるカジュアル レストラン"Bistro Terrace"
Left page, bottom, top / The casual restaurant "Bistro Terrace" equipped with a bar corner.

ラディソン プラザ ホテル & ゴルフコース
「ザ ラディソン ホテルズ」は北アメリカを中心に約90軒のチェーンを有
し フランス スイス スカンディナビアなどのホテルと関連チェーン
契約を持つなど 国際的にも展開している。中でも「ラディソン」と名の
付くホテルには"Hotel's""Plaza Hotels""Suite Hotels""Inns""Resorts"
といった異なるコンセプトの施設を設定し ビジネス客用 エグゼクテ
ィブ用や広々としたスイートルームを備えたもの ハイウェイやエアポ
ートの近くや リゾート地といったニードや立地などによってネーミン
グを区別している。
このホテルは ロサンゼルス国際空港より南へ約2.5マイルに位置するマ
ンハッタンビーチ地区に進出したもので 周辺にはオフィスが多い。ま
たゴルフコースを併設しているので ビジネスとレジャーを同時にエン
ジョイ出来る多目的ホテルとして エグゼクティブを中心に利用されて
いる。館内には フランス人シェフを迎えたレストラン「Califia」があり
宴会やパーティの利用も多い。
設計/Maxwell Starkman Associates
オープン/1986年8月
規模・客室数/地上8階建388室(内スイート18室)
料飲施設/4:Califia(レストラン)など
宴会・会議場/Manhattan Ballroom(6,784sq.-ft.) 中小宴会場 15室
その他の施設/ゴルフコース(9ホール) ヘルスクラブ サウナ プール
　　　　　　& スパ

RADISSON PLAZA HOTEL and Golf Course

"The Ladisson Hotels" chain has about 90 hotels mainly in North
America, and has concluded agreements related to chains of hotels
in France, Switzerland, Scandinavia, etc. "Radisson" hotels, among
others, are considered facilities with different concepts, such as
"Hotels," "Plaza Hotels," "Suite Hotels," "Inns" and "Resorts."
Different names are used, according to need, location, etc. There are
hotels for businessmen or executives, those with spacious suite rooms,
those near a highway or airport, those at a resort area.
This hotel has entered into the Manhattan Beach about 2.5 miles
south of Los Angeles International Airport, and there are many
offices can be found nearby. Since it is equipped with a golf course,
it is mainly used by executives as a multi-purpose hotel where guests
can enjoy both business and leisure activities. Inside the hotel building
is located "Califia," a restaurant managed by a French chef, while
often used for banquets or parties.

1400, Parkview Avenue, Manhattan Beach, CA 90266
Phone: 213-546-7511

Design / Architecture: Maxwell Starkman Associates
Opened / August, 1986
Scale, number of guest rooms / 8 stories, 388 rooms
　　(incl. 18 suite rooms)
Eating/drinking facilities / 4; Califia (restaurant), etc.
Banquet hall, boardroom / Manhattan Ballroom (6,784 sq. ft.),
　　Small- and medium-size banquet hall (15)
Other facilities / Golf course (9 holes), Health club, Sauna,
　　Pool & Spa

14世紀の女王のイメージより名付けたというフランス料理をベースにしたレストラン"Califia"（68席）
The restaurant "Califia" (68 seats) named after an image of a queen in the 14th century.

カジュアル レストラン"Bistro Terrace"
The casual restaurant "Bistro Terrace."

アート ビデオ レストラン"Waves"のバーカウンター
The bar counter of the art video restaurant "Waves."

ステージ状にレイアウトされた"Califia"

"Califia" featuring stage-like layout.

ダンスフロアを中央に設けたナイト スポット "Waves"

The night spot "Waves."

大宴会場"Manhattan Ballroom"(6,784sq.-ft.)

The large banquet hall "Manhattan Ballroom" (6,784 sq. ft.).

ゴルフコースに面した"Bistro Terrace"テラス ダイニング エリア

The terraced dining area of "Bistro Terrace" facing a golf course.

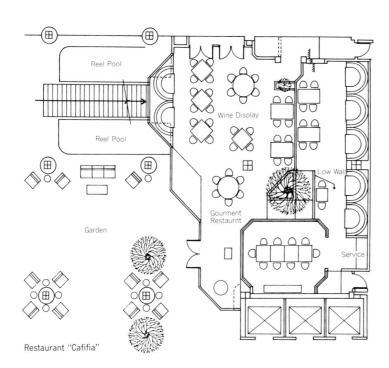

Reel Pool

Reel Pool

Wine Display

Low Wall

Garden

Gourment Restaurnt

Service

Restaurant "Cafifia"

上・下/18室あるスイートルームの一つ ウエットバーとパーラーが付いている

Top, bottom / One of the 18 suite rooms; equipped with a wet bar and parlor.

23エーカーの人造湖があるリゾートホテル
The resort hotel having an artificial lake (23 acres wide).

フロント レセプション エリア
The front reception area.

Ted Robinson の設計によるゴルフ場(18ホール)が2ヶ所
There are two golf courses designed by Ted Robinson.

12棟の建物で構成したホテルは892室の客室と13ヶ所の施設
The hotel, consisting of 12 buildings, has 892 rooms and 13 locations of facilities.

人造湖の中心部にある23,000sq.-ft.のプールと日光浴ビーチ
The 23,000 sq. ft. pool in the center of the artificial lake, and sunbathing beach.

MARRIOTT'S
DESERT SPRINGS

74-855 Country Club Drive Palm Desert, CA 92262
Phone/619-341-2211

232

メインレストラン"Lake View Restaurant"へのアプローチ
The approach to the main restaurant "Lake View Restaurant."

上・中・下/Lake View Restaurant" カリフォルニア＆ス
パ料理を提供する

Top, middle, bottom / "Lake View Restaurant" serves Californian spa dishes.

ボートのドッグを備えたアトリウム　　　　The atrium equipped with a boat dock.

マリオット デザート スプリングズ リゾート & スパ

総投資額2億5,000万ドル 工期 3年以上をかけ完成したこのホテルは 砂漠の中のオアシスともいえるリゾート都市 パームスプリングスより約13マイル南東に位置する。

アメリカの南西部における最も大きなコンベンションとリゾート施設を備えたホテルの一つで 375エーカーの広大な土地と共に23エーカーの人造湖を有し 12棟からなる建物で構成している。

892室の客室の他に 宴会及び会議室 ゴルフコース テニスコート ヘルススパ ショッピングアーケードなどがある。

広大な土地の自然とコンテンポラリィな建物との美しい調和をデザインしたのが 「Kahala Hilton」や「Maura Lani Resort」を担当した Killingsworth, Stricker, Lindgren, Wilson & Associates である。インテリアデザインは Jane Dillon が担当し 温かい ソフトなパステル調を強調し "果てしない地平線の印象" を創造することにあったとしている。

設計/建築・Killingsworth, Strickerer, Lindgren, Wilson
    & Associates
    内装・Jane Dillon
オープン/1987年2月18日
規模・客室数/12棟892室(内スイート 65室)
料飲施設/13(ダイニング及びエンターテイメント部門〔ファシリティ〕を含む)
宴会・会議場/大宴会場2 (25,000sq.-ft. 合計14室に分割可能及び20,000sq.-ft. 合計12室に分割可能) 会議室7室(内ボードルーム2室)
その他の施設/テニスコート16面 テニス クラブハウス&ショップ ゴルフコース2(各18ホール) ヘルス スパ (27,000sq.-ft.) プール クロケットコート ショッピングアーケード 美容 理容室
投資額/2億5,000万ドル

ゴルフをテーマしたグリルバーのレストラン"Club Room"

MARRIOTT'S DESERT SPRINGS Resort & Spa

With an investment of $250 million and 3 years spent for the construction, this hotel is situated about 13 miles southeast of Palm Springs, a resort city that is considered to be an oasis in the desert.

This hotel is one of such hotels equipped with the largest convention and resort facilities in the Southwest of America. Included within 375 acres of extensive land and 23 acres of artificial lake, it comprises 12 buildings. In addition to 892 rooms, there are banquet halls, conference rooms, golf courses, tennis courts, a health spa; a shopping arcade, etc. The designers, Killingsworth, Stricker, Lindgren, Wilson & Associates, have conceived a beautiful harmony between nature of extensive land and contemporary building, and they are the same designers who have undertaken the work for "Kahara Hilton," "Maura Lani Resort," etc. The interior design has been executed by Jane Dillon whose intention has been to stress warm, soft pastel coloring to create an "impression of endless horizon."

74-855, Country Club Drive, Palm Desert, CA 92262
Phone: 619-341-2211

Design / Architecture: Killingsworth, Stricker, Lindgren, Wilson & Associates
    Interior: Jane Dillon
Opened / February 18, 1987
Scale, number of guest rooms / 12 buildings, 892 rooms (incl. 65 suite rooms)
Eating/drinking facilities / 13 (incl. dining & entertainment departments (facilities))
Banquet hall, boardroom / Large banquet hall (one is 25,000 sq. ft. wide, divisible into 14 rooms; the other is 20,000 sq. ft. wide, divisible into 12 rooms), Conference room (7, including 2 boardrooms)
Other facilities / Tennis court (16), Tennis club house & shop, Golf course (2, having 18 holes each), Health spa (27,000 sq. ft.), Pool, Cricket court, Shopping arcade, Beauty parlor, Barber
Total investment / $250 million

各種専門店と売店は12,000sq.-ft. のスペースをもっている

(Photo captions)
Top / The grill & bar restaurant "Club Room" whose theme is golf.
Bottom / Various specialty shops and selling shops are open over 12,000 sq. ft. of space.

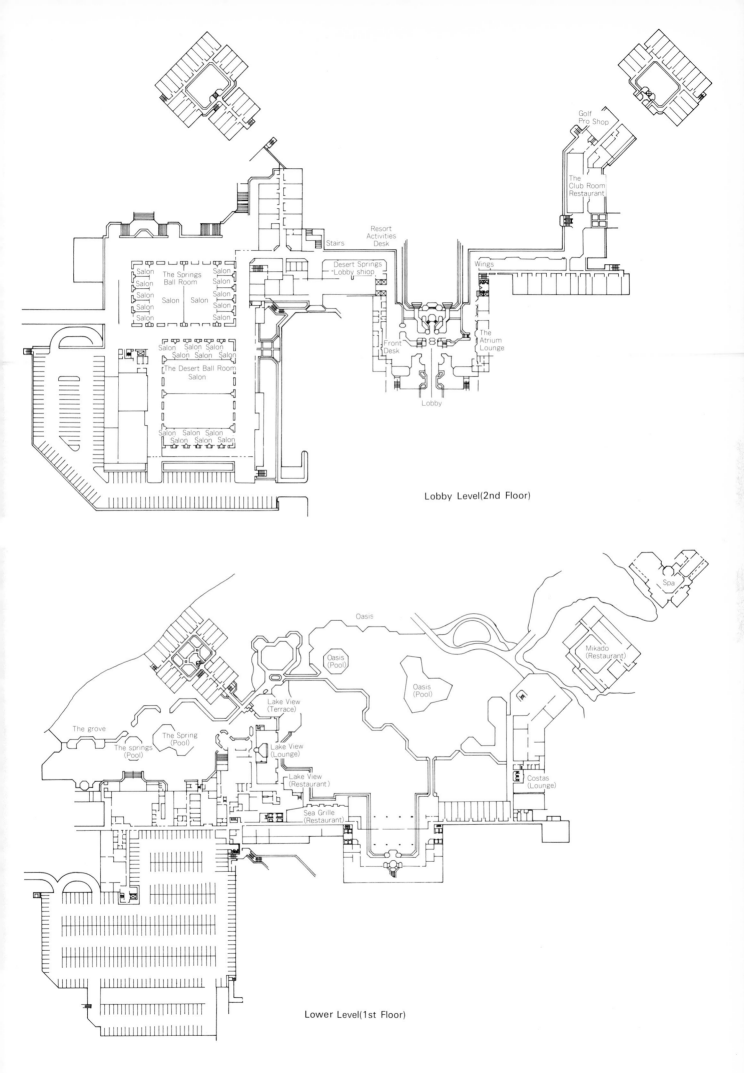

Lobby Level(2nd Floor)

Salon
Salon
Salon
Salon
Salon
The Springs Ball Room
Salon Salon
Salon
Salon
Salon
Salon
Salon
Salon Salon Salon
Salon Salon Salon
The Desert Ball Room
Salon
Salon Salon Salon
Salon Salon Salon

Stairs
Resort Activities Desk
Desert Springs Lobby shop
Front Desk
Lobby
Wings
The Atrium Lounge
The Club Room Restaurant
Golf Pro Shop

Lower Level(1st Floor)

Oasis
Oasis (Pool)
Oasis (Pool)
Lake View (Terrace)
The grove
The Spring (Pool)
The springs (Pool)
Lake View (Lounge)
Lake View (Restaurant)
Sea Grille (Restaurant)
Costas (Lounge)
Mikado (Restaurant)
Spa

大宴会場(25,000sq.-ft.)は14室に区分できる
The large banquet hall (25,000 sq. ft.) can be divided into 14 rooms.

ナイト スポット"Costa's"のラウンジ&バーカウンター

オープンキッチンを設けたシーフードレストラン"Sea Grill"
The seafood restaurant "Sea Grill," provided with an open kitchen.

"Sea Grill"のファサード　The facade of "Sea Grill."

The lounge & bar counter of the night spot "Costa's."

アトリウムに面した"Atrium Lounge"　　"Atrium Lounge" facing the atrium.

ヘルス スパ内のジムの装備　Gymnasium equipment within the health spa.

別棟にあるヘルスセンター内のヘアデザイン店"Jose Eber of Beverly Hills"

The hair design shop "**Jose Eber** of Beverly Hills" within the health center in a separate building."

トータルで51,300sq.-ft.の宴会場と会議場施設も売り物のひとつ
The banquet halls and conference hall facilities, 51,300 sq. ft. in total, are among the attractive features of this hotel.

スパに併設した屋外プール

The outdoor pool attached to the spa.

スパにあるサウナと水療法（Hydrotnerapy）の施設
The sauna and hydrotherapy equipment at the spa.

夜間照明付きのテニスコートが16面ある
There are 16 tennis courts with night lighting equipment.

上・下／31,500sq.ft. のプレジデンシャル スイートルーム

Top, bottom / "Presidential Suite Room" (31,500 sq. ft.).